Bibliographies for Biblical Research

New Testament Series

in Twenty-One Volumes

General Editor

Watson E. Mills

Bibliographies for Biblical Research

New Testament Series

in Twenty-One Volumes

Volume XII

Colossians

Compiled by

Watson E. Mills

MELLEN BIBLICAL PRESS

Lewiston/Queenston/Lampeter

Library of Congress Cataloging-in-Publication Data

Bibliographies for biblical research.

Includes index.
Contents: v. 1. The Gospel of Matthew / compiled by
Watson E. Mills --   -- v. 12. Colossians
1. Bible. N.T.--Criticism, interpretation, etc.--
Bibliography.   I. Mills, Watson E.

Z7772.L1B4 1993 [BS2341.2]   016.2262'06   93-30864

ISBN 0-7734-2347-8 (v. 1) Matthew   ISBN 0-7734-2349-4 (v. 2) Mark
ISBN 0-7734-2385-0 (v. 3) Luke   ISBN 0-7734-2357-5 (v. 4) John
ISBN 0-7734-2432-6 (v. 5) Acts   ISBN 0-7734-2418-0 (v. 6) Romans
ISBN 0-7734-2419-9 (v. 7) 1 Corinthians ISBN 0-7734-2442-3 (v. 8) 2 Corinthians
ISBN 0-7734-2468-7 (v. 9) Galatians ISBN 0-7734-2472-5 (v. 10) Ephesians
ISBN 0-7734-2474-1 (v. 11) Philippians ISBN 0-7734-2476-8 (v. 12) Colossians
ISBN 0-7734-2438-5 (v. 21) Revelation

This is volume 12 in the continuing series
Bibliographies for Biblical Research
New Testament Series
Volume 12 ISBN 0-7734-2476-8
Series ISBN 0-7734-9345-X

A CIP catalog record for this book is available from the British Library.

Copyright © 1999 The Edwin Mellen Press

The Edwin Mellen Press   The Edwin Mellen Press
Box 450   Box 67
Lewiston, New York   Queenston, Ontario
USA 14092   CANADA L0S 1L0

Edwin Mellen Press, Ltd.
Lampeter, Dyfed, Wales
UNITED KINGDOM SA48 7DY

Printed in the United States of America

Dedication

In memory of my maternal grandmother

Mary Sue West Watson

1873-1927

with great appreciation and affection

Contents

Introduction to the Series

This volume is the twelfth in a series of bibliographies on the books of the Hebrew and Christian Bibles as well as the deutero-canonicals. This ambitious series calls for some 35-40 volumes over the next 3-5 years compiled by practicing scholars from various traditions.

Each author (compiler) of these volumes is working within the general framework adopted for the series, i.e., citations are to works published within the twentieth century that make important contributions to the understanding of the text and backgrounds of the various books.

Obviously the former criterion is more easily quantifiable than the latter, and it is precisely at this point that an individual compiler makes her/his specific contribution. We are not intending to be comprehensive in the sense of definitive, but where resources are available, as many listings as possible have been included.

The arrangement for the entries, in most volumes in the series, consists of three divisions: scriptural citations; subject citations; commentaries. In some cases the first two categories may duplicate each other to some degree. Multiple citations by scriptural citation are also included where relevant.

Those who utilize these volumes are invited to assist the compilers by noting textual errors as well as obvious omissions that ought to be taken into account in subsequent printings. Perfection is nowhere more elusive than in the citation of bibliographic materials. We would welcome your assistance at this point.

When the series is completed, the entire contents of all volumes (updated) will be available on CD-ROM. This option will be available, without charge, to those who have subscribed to the casebound volumes.

We hope that these bibliographies will contribute to the discussions and research going on in the field among faculty as well as students. They should serve a significant role as reference works in both research and public libraries.

I wish to thank the staff and editors of the Edwin Mellen Press, and especially Professor Herbert Richardson, for the gracious support of this series.

Watson E. Mills, Series Editor
Mercer University
Macon GA 31211
January 2000

Preface

This Bibliography on the Epistle to the Colossians provides an index to the journal articles, essays in collected works, books and monographs and commentaries published in the twentieth century through the early months of 1999. Technical works of scholarship, from many differing traditions constitute the bulk of the citations though I have included some selected works that intend to reinterpret this research to a wider audience.

I acknowledge the work of Paul-Émile Langevin, *Bibliographie biblique* (Les Presses de l'Université Laval, 1972, 1978, 1985). This work is especially useful in verifying Catholic publications particularly citations to French literature. These volumes are meticulously indexed by scriptural citation as well as subject. Building the database necessary for a work of this magnitude was a tedious and time-consuming task. I acknowledge with gratitude the Education Commission of the Southern Baptist Convention which provided funds for travel to overseas libraries during the summers of 1994, 1995 and 1999, as well as Mercer University which also funded some of the travel costs.

I want to express my gratitude to the staff librarians at the following institutions: Baptist Theological Seminary (Rüschlikon, Switzerland); Oxford

University   (Oxford, UK); Emory University (Atlanta, GA); Duke University (Durham, NC); University of Zürich (Zürich, Switzerland); Southern Baptist Theological Seminary (Louisville, KY).

Watson E. Mills
Mercer University
Macon GA 31207
January 2000

Abbreviations

AfER	African Ecclesial Review (Masaka, Uganda)
AL	Archiv für Liturgiewissenschaft (W. Maria Laach, Germany)
Ant	Antonianum (Rome)
AsiaJT	The Asia Journal of Theology (Bangalore)
AsSeign	Assemblees du Seigneur (Brugge; Paris)
AUSS	Andrews University Seminary Studies (Berrien Springs, MI)
BI	Biblical Illustrator (Nashville, TN)
Bib	Biblica (Rome)
BibL	Bibel und Leben (Düsseldorf)
BibO	Bibbia e Oriente (Milan)
Bij	Bijdragen (Nijmegen)
BJRL	Bulletin of the John Rylands University Library (Manchester)
BR	Biblical Research (Chicago)
BTB	Biblical Theology Bulletin (Jamaica NY)
BVC	Bible et Vie Chretienne (Paris)
BZ	Biblische Zeitschrift (Paderborn)
CahEv	Cahiers Évangile (Paris)

CANZTR	Colloquium: The Australian and New Zealand Theological Review (Auchland)
CBQ	Catholic Biblical Quarterly (Washington, DC)
CEJ	Christian Education Journal (Glen Ellyn IL)
Chr	Christus (Paris)
CICR	Communio: International Catholic Review (Spokane, WA)
CQ	Covenant Quarterly (Chicago)
Crux	Crux (Vancouver)
CThM	Currents in Theology and Mission (St. Louis, MO)
CTJ	Calvin Theological Journal (Grand Rapids, MI)
CTM	Concordia Theological Monthly (St. Louis, MO)
CTQ	Concordia Theological Quarterly (Fort Wayne, IN)
Dia	Dialog (Minneapolis, MN)
Did	Didascalia (Rosario)
EE	Estudios Eclesiásticos (Madrid)
EQ	Evangelical Quarterly (London)
ERT	Evangelical Review of Theology (New Delhi)
ET	Expository Times (Edinburgh)
ETR	Etudes Théologiques et Religieuses (Montpellier)
EV	Esprit et Vie (Langres)
EvT	Evangelische Theologie (Munich)
FM	Faith and Mission (Wake Forest, NC)
Found	Foundations (Rochester, NY)
FundJ	Fundamentalist Journal (Lynchburg, VA)
FV	Foi et Vie (Paris)
GeistL	Geist und Leben (Würzburg)
Greg	Gregorianum (Rome)
GTJ	Grace Theological Journal (Winona Lake, IN)
HTR	Harvard Theological Review (Cambridge, MA)

HTS	Hervormde Teologiese Studies (Pretoria)
IJT	Indian Journal of Theology (Serampore)
IKaZ	Internationale Katholische Zeitschrift (Communio: Rodenkirchen)
Int	Interpretation (Richmond, VA)
JBL	Journal of Biblical Literature (Atlanta, GA)
JDharma	Journal of Dharma (Bangalore)
JETS	Journal of the Evangelical Theological Society (Wheaton, IL)
JmosP	Journal of the Moscow Patriarchate (Moscow)
JPT	Journal of Psychology and Theology (La Mirada, CA)
JRE	Journal of Religious Ethics (Knoxville TN)
JSNT	Journal for the Study of the New Testament (Sheffield)
JTS	Journal of Theological Studies (Oxford)
JTSA	Journal of Theology for Southern Africa (Rondebosch)
KD	Kerygma and Dogma (Göttingen)
LTQ	Lutheran Theological Quarterly (Gettysburg PA)
MidS	Mid-Stream (Indianapolis)
MS	Mission Studies (Leiden)
NovT	Novum Testamentum (Leiden)
NRT	La Nouvelle revue théologique (Louvain)
NTS	New Testament Studies (Cambridge)
OC	One in Christ (Turvey, Bedfordshire)
Point	Point (Papua, New Guinea)
Pres	Presbyterion (St. Louis)
PRS	Perspectives in Religious Studies (Macon, GA)
QR	Quarterly Review (Nashville TN)
RechSR	Recherches de science religieuse (Paris)
Reformatio	Reformatio: Evangelische Zeitschrift für Kultur und Politik (Zürich)
Rel	Religion: A Journal of Religion and Religions (London)
RevExp	Review and Expositor (Louisville, KY)

RevRéf	Revue réformée (Saint-Germain-en-Laye)
RevSR	Revue des Sciences religieuses (Strasbourg)
RHPR	Revue d'histoire et de philosophie religieuses (Strasbourg)
RivBib	Rivista Biblica (Brescia)
RQ	Restoration Quarterly (Austin, TX)
RS	Religion and Society: Bulletin of the Christian Institute for the Study of Religion and Society (Bangalore, India)
RSB	Religious Studies Bulletin (Calgary)
RSPT	Revue des Sciences Philosophiques et Thélogiques (Paris)
RT	Revue Thomiste (Paris)
RTR	Reformed Theological Review (Melbourne)
SBFLA	Studii Biblici Franciscani Liber Annuus (Jerusalem)
SBLSP	Society of Biblical Literature Seminar Papers (Atlanta)
SBT	Studia Biblica et Theologica (Pasadena, CA)
ScE	Science et Esprit (Montreal)
ScripT	Scripta theologia (Pamplona, Spain)
SE	Sciences Ecclésiastiques (Montreal)
SEÅ	Svensk Exegetisk Årsbok (Lund)
SEAJT	South East Asia Journal of Theology (Singapore)
SEcu	Studi Ecumenici (Verona)
SJT	Scottish Journal of Theology (Edinburgh)
SouJT	Southwestern Journal of Theology (Fort Worth TX)
StTheol	Studia Theologica (Copenhagen)
StudB	Studia biblica (Berlin)
StudE	Studia evangelica (Berlin)
SVTQ	St. Vladimir's Theological Quarterly (New York)
TGl	Theologie und Glaube (Paderborn, Germany)
Theology	Theology (London)
ThEv	Theologia evangelica (Pretoria)

TLZ	Theologische Literaturzeitung (Leipzig)
TQ	Theologische Quartalschift (Tübingen)
TriJ	Trinity Journal (Deerfield, IL)
TS	Theological Studies (Woodstock)
TynB	Tyndale Bulletin (Cambridge)
TZ	Theologische Zeitschrift (Basel)
VD	Verbum Domine (Rome)
VerbC	Verbum Caro: Revue théologique et oecuménique (Neuchâtel)
VoxE	Vox evangelica (London)
VS	La vie spirituelle (Paris)
Way	Way (London)
WTJ	Westminster Theology Journal (Philadelphia)
WW	Word and World (St. Paul MN)
ZNW	Zeitschrift für die neutestamentliche Wissenschaft (Berlin)
ZTK	Zeitschrift für Theologie und Kirche (Tübingen)
Zygon	Zygon: Journal of Religion and Science (Chicago)

PART ONE

Citations by Chapter and Verse

0001 G. Giavini, "Riflessi della cristologia di Col. 1 sulla lettura di Gen. 1-3," in *La Cristologia in san Paolo*. Brescia: Paideia, 1976. Pp. 257-67.

0002 F. Zeillinger, "Versöhnung - Gedanken zum Kolosserbrief," *BibL* 49 (1976): 434-37.

0003 Michel Bouttier, "Petite suite paulinienne," *ETR* 60 (1985): 265-72.

1:1-28

0004 Robert Paul Roth, "Christ and the Powers of Darkness: Lessons from Colossians," *WW* 6 (1986): 336-44.

1:1-14

0005 Isolde K. Anderson, "Somebody's Something," *CQ* 43 (1985): 11-15.

0006 T. R. Gildmeister, "Christology and the Focus of Faith: Readings from Paul's Letter to the Colossians in Year C," *QR* 18 (1998): 89-110.

1:1-8

0007 Eduard Lohse, "Die Mitarbeiter des Apostels Paulus im Kolosserbrief ," in O. Böcher and K. Haacker, eds., *Verborum Veritas* (festschrift for Gustav Stählin). Wuppertal: Brockhaus, 1970. Pp. 189-94.

1:3-3:4

0008 L. Ramaroson, "Structure de Colossiens 1:3-3:4," *SE* 29 (1977): 313-19.

1:3-11

0009 Z. Kiernikowski, "Identitià e dinamisnlo della vita cristiana secondo Col. 1:3-11," *RivBib* 33 (1985): 63-79; 191-228.

1:3-12

0010 J. G. van der Watt, "Colossians 1:3-12 Considered as an Exordium," *JTSA* 57 (1986): 32-42.

1:4-6

0011 Daniel C. Stevens, "Christian Educational Foundations and the Pauline Triad: A Call to Faith, Hope, and Love," *CEJ* 5 (1984): 5-16.

1:7

0012 Carl Diemer, "Deacons and Other Endangered Species: A Look at the Biblical Office of Deacon," *FundJ* 3 (1984): 21-24.

1:9-2:3
> **0013** J. O'Neill, "The Source of Christology in Colossians," *NTS* 26 (1979-1980): 87-100.

1:9-19
> **0014** O. A. Piper, "The Savior's Eternal Work. An Exegesis of Colossians 1:9-29," *Int* 3 (1949): 286-98.

1:9-12
> **0015** G. T. Montague, "The Christian Bears Fruit and Grows: Colossians 1:9-12," in *Growth in Christ*. Kirkwood: Maryhurst Press, 1961. Pp. 69-80.

1:9
> **0016** Bernardo M. Antonini, "La conoscenza della volontà di Dio in Col. 1,9b," in *La Cristologia in san Paolo*. Brescia: Paideia, 1976. Pp. 301-40.

> **0017** Leopold Sabourin, "Paul and His Thought in Recent Research," *RSB* 2 (1982): 62-73; 3 (1983): 117-31.

> **0018** Henri Crouzel, "Die Spiritualität des Origenes: Ihre Bedeutung für die Gegenwart," *TQ* 165 (1985): 132-42.

1:11-19
> **0019** Stanley J. Samartha, "Religion, Culture and Power - Three Bible Studies," *RS* 34 (1987): 66-79.

1:12-24
> **0020** Jean Perret, "Notes bibliques de prédication sur trois péricopes de l'Épître de saint Paul aux Colossiens," *VerbC* 19 (1965): 57-64.

1:12-20
> **0021** P. Menoud, "Col. 1: 12-20," *ETR* 30 (1955): 5-8.

> **0022** P. Lamarche, "La primauté du Christ," *AsSeign* NS 46 (1974): 59-64.

> **0023** W. R. G. Loader, "The Apocalyptic Model of Sonship: Its Origin and Development in New Testament Tradition," *JBL* 97 (1978): 525-54.

> **0024** Hartmut Löwe, "Bekenntnis, Apostelamt und Kirche im Kolosserbrief," in Dieter Lührmann and Georg Strecker, eds., *Kirche*

(festschrift for Günther Bornkamm). Tübingen: Mohr, 1980. Pp. 299-314.

0025 T. Evan Pollard, "Colossians 1:12-20: A Reconsideration," *NTS* 27 (1980-1981): 572-75.

0026 David H. Tripp, "The Colossian 'Hymn': Seeking a Version to Praise with," *OC* 26 (1990): 231-37.

0027 Rudolf Hoppe, "Theologie in den Deuteropaulinen," in Hans J. Klauck, ed., *Monotheismus und Christologie: zur Gottesfrage im hellenistischen Judentum und im Urchristentum*. Freiburg: Herder, 1992. Pp. 163-86.

1:12-14

0028 H. Halter, "Col 1,12-14. Errettet aus dem Machtbereich der Finsternis, erlöst im Lichtreich des Sohnes," in *Taufe und Ethos: Paulinische Kriterien für das Proprium christlicher Moral*. Freiburg: Herder, 1977. Pp. 183-90.

0029 Gary S. Shogren, "Presently Entering the Kingdom of Christ: The Background and Purpose of Colossians 1:12-14," *JETS* 31 (1988): 173-80.

1:12-13

0030 R. Schnackenburg, "Aus Dunkel zurn Licht (Kol 1,12-13)," in *Glaubensimpulse aus dem Neuen Testament*. Düsseldorf: Patmos, 1972. Pp. 118-22.

1:13-29

0031 P. D. Kessler, "Er hat uns errettet," *BibL* 41 (1968): 33-36.

1:13-20

0032 J. M. Bissen, "De primatu Christi absoluto apud Coloss. 1,13-20," *Ant* 11 (1936): 3-26.

0033 D. M. Stanley, "A Hymn from the Early Christian Liturgy. Colossians 1:13-20," in *Christ's Resurrection in Pauline Soteriology*. Rome: Pontifical Institute Press, 1961. Pp. 202-208.

0034 F.-X. Durrwell, "Le Christ, premier et dernier," *BVC* 54 (1963): 16-28

0035   John Behr, "Colossians 1:13-20: A Chiastic Reading," *SVTQ* 40 (1996): 247-64.

0036   J. H. Roberts, "Die belydenisuitspraak Kolossense 1:13-20," *HTS* 53 (1997): 476-97.

1:13

0037   F. Ogara, "Qui nos transtulit in regnum Filii dilectionis suae," *VD* 17 (1937): 296-302.

0038   T. Torrance, "The Pre-eminence of Jesus Christ," *ET* 89 (1977): 54-55.

1:14-20

0039   C. Casale Marcheselli, "La struttura letteraria di Col 1,(14b).15-20a.b.1.2. La celebrazione cultuale della funzionalità ministeriale del primato-servizio di Gesù Cristo Signore," in *Parola e Spirito*. Brescia: Paideia, 1982. 497-519.

0040   C. Casale Marcheselli, "La comunità cristiana di Colossi esprime la sua fede in Gesù Cristo," *RivBib* 31 (1983): 273-91.

1:15-28

0041   T. R. Gildmeister, "Christology and the Focus of Faith: Readings from Paul's Letter to the Colossians in Year C," *QR* 18 (1998): 89-110.

1:15-23

0042   Daniel von Allmen, "Réconciliation du monde et christologie cosmique de 2 Cor 5:14-21 à Col 1:15-23," *RHPR* 48 (1968): 32-45.

0043   Colin Gunton, "Atonement and the Project of Creation: An Interpretation of Colossians 1:15-23," *Dia* 35 (1996): 35-41.

1:15-20

0044   S. de Ausejo, "Es un himno a Cristo el prólogo de San Juan? Los himnos cristologicos de la Iglesia primitiva y el prólogo del IV Evangelio Qn., 1, 18," in *La escatología individual neotestamentaria a la luz de las ideas en los tiempos apostolicos*. Madrid: Liberia, 1956. Pp. 307-96.

0045   J. M. Robinson, "A Formal Analysis of Colossians 1:15-20," *JBL* 76 (1957): 270-87.

0046 Werner Förster, "Die Grundzüge der Ptolemäischen Gnosis," *NTS* 6 (1959-1960): 16-31.

0047 J. Jervell, "Zu Kol 1,15-20. Gott in Christus II," in *Imago Dei: Gen 1.26f im Spätjudentum, in der Gnosis und in den paulinischen Briefen.* FRLANT #76. Göttingen: Vandenhoeck & Ruprecht, 1960. Pp. 218-26.

0048 Ernst Bammel, "Versuch zu Col 1,15-20," *ZNW* 52 (1961): 88-95.

0049 Harald Hegermann, *Die Vorstellung vom Schopfungsmittler im hellinistischen Judentum und Urchristentum.* Berlin, Akademie-Verlag, 1961.

0050 Paul Ellingworth, "Colossians i. 15-20 and Its Context," *ET* 73 (1961-1962): 252-53.

0051 James H. Burtness, "All the Fulness," *Dia* 3 (1964): 257-63.

0052 G. W. H. Lampe, "New Testament Doctrine of *Ktisis*," *SJT* 17 (1964): 449-62.

0053 Ralph P. Martin, "An Early Christian Hymn," *EQ* 36 (1964): 195-205.

0054 H. Bürke, "Die Frage nach dem kosmischen Christus als Beispiel einer ökumenisch orientierten Theologie," *KD* 11 (1965): 103-15.

0055 H. J. Gabathuler, *Jesus Christus. Haupt der Kirche - Haupt der Welt. Der Christushymnus Colosser 1, 15-20 in der theologischen Forschung der letzten 130 Jahre.* ATANT #45. Zürich, Zwingli, 1965.

0056 E. Käsemann, "Eine urchristliche Taufliturgie," in *Exegetische Versuche und Besinnungen.* Göttingen: Vandenhoech & Ruprecht, 1965. 34-51.

0057 Kurt Scharf, "Scope of the Redemptive Task, Colossians 1:15-20," *CTM* 36 (1965): 291-300.

0058 Fred B. Craddock, " 'All Things in Him': A Critical Note on Colossians 1:15-20," *NTS* 12 (1965-1966): 78-80.

0059   A. F. Thompson, "The Colossian Vision in Theology and Philosophy,"
       IJT 15 (1966): 121-29.

0060   R. Deichgräber, "Kolosser 1, 15-20," in *Gotteshymnus und
       Christushymmis in der frühen Christenheit: Untersuchungen zu
       Form, Sprache und Stil der frühchristlichen Hymnus.* Göttingen:
       Vandenhoeck & Ruprecht, 1967. Pp. 143-55.

0061   E. Testa, "Gesù pacificatore universale," *SBFLA* 19 (1969): 5-64.

0062   A. Vögtle, "Der Christushymnus Kol 1, 15-20," in *Das Neue
       Testament und die Zukunft des Kosmos.* Düsseldorf: Patmos, 1970.
       Pp. -33.

0063   John G. Gibbs, "Colossians 1: 15-20," in *Creation and Redemption:
       A Study in Pauline Theology.* Leiden: Brill, 1971. Pp. 94-114.

0064   J. T. Sanders, *The New Testament Christological Hymns: Their
       Historical-Religious Background.* Cambridge: University Press, 1971.
       Pp. 12-14, 75-87.

0065   B. Vawter, "The Colossians Hymn and the Principle of Redaction,"
       CBQ 33 (1971): 62-81.

0066   Roy A. Harrisville, "Der kosmische Christus im Neuen Testament,"
       in V. Vajta, ed., *Das Evangelium und die Bestimmung des Menschen.*
       Göttingen: Vandenhoeck & Ruprecht, 1972. Pp. 38-63.

0067   Eduard Schweizer, "Lord of the Nations," *SEAJT* 13 (1972): 13-21.

0068   Wolfgang Pöhlmann, "Die hymnischen All-Prädikationen in Kol
       1:15-20," *ZNW* 64 (1973): 53-74.

0069   Beda Rigaux, "Col 1,15-20," in *Dieu l'a ressuscité: Exégèse et
       théologie biblique.* Gembloux: Duculot, 1973. Pp. 154-58.

0070   F. Zeillinger, *Der Erstgeborene der Schöpfung. Unter suchungen zur
       Formul Formalstruktur und Theologie des Kolos serbriefes.* Vienna:
       Herder, 1974.

0071   Pierre Benoit, "L'hymne christologique de Col. 1,15-20. Jugement
       critique sur l'état des recherches," in Jacob Neusner, ed., *Christianity,*

Judaism and Other Greco-Roman Cults (festschrift for Morton Smith) Part One. Leiden: Brill, 1975. Pp. 226-63.

0072 C. Burger, "Der Hymnus in Kolosser 1,15-20," in *Schöpfung und Versöhnung*. Neukrichen-Vluyn: Neukrichener Verlag, 1975. Pp. 3-114.

0073 C. Burger, *Schöpfung und Versöhnung: Studien zum liturgischen Gui im Kolosser- und Epheserbrief.* WMANT #46. Neukirchen-Vluyn: Neukirchener, 1975.

0074 E. H. Maly, "Creation in the New Testament," in Miriam Ward, ed., *Biblical Studies in Contemporary Thought.* Burlington VT: Trinity College Biblical Institute, 1975. Pp. 104-12.

0075 J.-N. Aletti, "Créés dans le Christ," *Chr* 23 (1976): 343-56.

0076 P. Dacquino, "Cristo Figlio di Dio e Figlio dell'Uomo," in *Studia Hiorosolyrnitana. I. Studi archeologici* (festschrift for Bellarmino Bagatti). Jerusalem: Francisan Press, 1976. Pp. 135-45.

0077 A. di Giovanni, "Impianto teoretico e struttura dialettica di Col. 1, 15-20," in *La Cristologia in san Paolo.* Brescia: Paideia, 1976. Pp. 247-56.

0078 P. Grech, "L'inno cristologico di Col. 1 e la gnosi," in *La Cristologia in san Paolo.* Brescia: Paideia, 1976. Pp. 81-95.

0079 Stanislas Lyonnet, "Ruolo cosmico di Cristo in Col. 1, 15ss. in luce di quello della Tora nel giudaismo," in *La Cristologia in san Paolo.* Brescia: Paideia, 1976. Pp. 57-79.

0080 F. Montagnini, "Linee di convergenza fra la sapienza vetertestamentaria e l'inno cristologico di Col. 1," in *La Cristologia in san Paolo.* Brescia: Paideia, 1976. Pp. 37-56

0081 P. Rossano, "Riflessi ecumenici di Cristo secondo Col. 1, 15-20," in *La Cristologia in san Paolo.* Brescia: Paideia, 1976. Pp. 382-84.

0082 G. Segalla, "L'inno cristologico di Col. 1,15-20 nel quadro degli altri inni e della cristologia paolina," in *La Cristologia in san Paolo.* Brescia: Paideia, 1976. Pp. 375-77.

0083   Tito Szabó, "La croce del primogenito: il primato della croce nel piano divino della creazione," in Christian Duquoc, et al., eds., *La sapienza della croce oggi, 1: la sapienza della croce nella rivelazione e nell'ecumenismo*. Turin: Elle Di Ci, 1976. Pp. 210-23.

0084   F. Manns, "Col. 1,15-20 inidrash chrétien de Gen. 1,1," *RevSR* 53 (1979): 100-10.

0085   Wayne McCown, "The Hymnic Structure of Colossians 1:15-20," *EQ* 51 (1979): 156-62.

0086   J.-N. Aletti, "Colossien 1,15-20," *CahEv* NS 32 (1980): 54-61.

0087   J.-N. Aletti, *Colossiens 1:15-20. Genre et exégèse du texte. Fonction de la thématique sapientielle*. Analecta Biblica #91. Rome: Biblical Institute Press, 1981.

0088   Markus Barth, "Christ and All Things," in Morna D. Hooker and Stephen G. Wilson, eds., *Paul and Paulinism* (festschrift for C. K. Barrett). London: SPCK, 1982. Pp. 160-72.

0089   Roland Bergmeier, "Königlosigkeit als nachvalentinianisches Heilsprädikat," *NovT* 24 (1982): 316-39.

0090   Larry R. Helyer, "Colossians 1:15-20: Pre-Pauline or Pauline?" *JETS* 26 (1983): 167-79.

0091   G. E. Long, "The Economy of Grace," *ET* 95 (1983): 17-18.

0092   Wolfgang Schenk, "Christus, das Geheimnis der Welt, als dogmatisches und ethisches Grundprinzip des Kolosserbriefes," *EvT* 43 (1983): 138-55.

0093   Gedaliahu A. G. Stroumsa, "Form(s) of God: Some Notes on *Metatron* and Christ," *HTR* 76 (1983): 269-88.

0094   F. F. Bruce, "Colossian Problems: The 'Christ Hymn' of Colossians 1:15-20," *BSac* 141 (1984): 99-111.

0095   Ingvild S. Gilhus, "The Gnostic Demiurge: An Agnostic Trickster," *Rel* 14 (1984): 301-11.

0096 Philip J. Hefner, "God and Chaos: The Demiurge Versus the Ungrund," *Zygon* 19 (1984): 469-85.

0097 Gerald H. Anderson, "Christian Mission and Human Transformation: Toward Century 21," *MS* 2 (1985): 52-65.

0098 John F. Balchin, "Colossians 1:15-20: An Early Christian Hymn? The Arguments from Style," *VoxE* 15 (1985): 65-94.

0099 Steven M. Baugh, "The Poetic Form of Colossians 1:15-20," *WTJ* 47 No 2 (1985): 227-44.

0100 Anne Etienne, "Réconciliation: un aspect de la théologie paulinienne," *FV* 84 (1985):49-57.

0101 Franz Mussner, "Das Reich Christi: Bemerkungen zur Eschatologie des Corpus Paulinum," in Michael Böhnke and Hanspeter Heinz, eds., *Im Gespräch mit dem dreieinen Gott: Elemente einer trinitarischen Theologie* (festschrift for Wilhelm Breuning). Düsseldorf: Patmos Verlag, 1985. Pp. 141-55.

0102 Eduard Schweizer, "Unterwegs mit meinen Lehrern," *EvT* 45 (1985): 322-37.

0103 Jan Botha, "A Stylistic Analysis of the Christ Hymn (Col 1:15-20)," in Kobus J. H. Petzer and Patrick J. Hartin, eds., *A South African Perspective on the New Testament* (festschrift for Bruce M. Metzger). Leiden: E. J. Brill, 1986. Pp. 238-51.

0104 Antonio Orbe, "Deus facit, homo fit: un axioma de san Ireneo," *Greg* 69 (1988): 629-61.

0105 Eduard Schweizer, "Zur Frage der Gotteserkenntnis in ausserchristlichen Religionen," in Jochanan Hesse, ed., *"Mitten im Tod - vom Leben Umfangen"* (festschrift for Werner Kohler. Frankfurt: Peter Lang, 1988. Pp. 236-39.

0106 Nikolaus Walter, "Geschichte und Mythos in der urchristlichen Präexistenzchristologie," in Hans H. Schmid, ed., *Mythos und Rationalität*. Gütersloh: Gütersloher Verlaghaus Mohn, 1988. Pp. 224-34.

0107   Jan Botha, "Die Kolossense-himne (Kol 1:15-20)," *HTS* suppl 1 (1989): 54-82.

0108   Jarl Fossum, "Colossians 1:15-18a in the Light of Jewish Mysticism and Gnosticism," *NTS* 35 (1989): 183-201.

0109   Michel Gourgues, "La foi chrétienne primitive face à la croix: le témoignage des formulaires pré-pauliniens," *ScE* 41 (1989): 49-69.

0110   Hugolinus Langkammer, "Jesus in der Sprache der neutestamentlichen Christuslieder," in Hubert Frankemölle and Karl Kertelge, eds., *Vom Urchristentum zu Jesus* (festschrift for Joachim Gnilka). Freiburgi: Herder, 1989. Pp. 467-86.

0111   Joseph Sittler, "Called to Unity," *CThM* 16 (1989): 5-13.

0112   Artemio M. Zabala, "Advent Reflections on Colossians 1:15-20," *AsiaJT* 3 (1989): 315-29.

0113   Edgar Haulotte, "Formation du corpus du Nouveau Testament: recherche d'un 'module' génératif intratextuel," in Christoph Theobald, ed., *Le canon des Ecritures: études historiques, exégétiques et systématiques.* Paris: Editions du Cerf, 1990. Pp. 255-439.

0114   Eduard Schweizer, "Colossians 1:15-20," *RevExp* 87 (1990): 97-104.

0115   Walter Wink, "The Hymn of the Cosmic Christ," in Robert T. Fortna and Beverly R. Gaventa, eds., *The Conversation Continues: Studies in Paul & John* (festschrift for Louis Martyn). Nashville: Abingdon Press, 1990. Pp. 235-45.

0116   N. T. Wright, "Poetry and Theology in Colossians 1:15-20," *NTS* 36 (1990): 444-68.

0117   Andrew Chester, "Jewish Messianic Expectations and Mediatorial Figures and Pauline Christology," in Martin Hengel and Ulrich Heckel, eds., *Paulus und das antike Judentum* (festschriftr for Adolf Schlatter). Tübingen: Mohr, 1991. Pp. 17-89.

0118   Larry R. Helyer, "Recent Research on Colossians 1:15-20," *GTJ* 12 (1991): 51-67.

0119   Richard J. Clifford, "The Bible and the Environment," in Kevin W. Irwin and Edmund D. Pellegrino, eds., *Preserving the Creation: Environmental Theology and Ethics*. Washington: Georgetown University Press, 1994. Pp. 1-26.

0120   Larry R. Helyer, "Cosmic Christology and Colossians 1:15-20," *JETS* 37 (1994): 235-46.

0121   Robert J. Karris, *A Symphony of New Testament Hymns: Commentary on Philippians 2:5-11, Colossians 1:15-20, Ephesians 2:14-16, 1 Timothy 3:16, Titus 3:4-7, 1 Peter 3:18-22, and 2 Timothy 2:11-13*. Collegeville MN: Liturgical Press, 1996.

0122   Harold Broeckhoven, "The Social Profiles in the Colossian Debate," *JSNT* 66 (1997): 73-90.

0123   C. Basevi, "Col 1:15-20: Las posibles fuentes del 'himmo' cristológico y su importamcia para la interpretación," *ScripT* 30 (1998): 779-802.

0124   P. Jones, "L'Évangile pour l'âge du verseau: Colossiens 1:15-20," *RefRéf* 50 (1999): 13-23.

1:15-18

0125   B. R. Brinkman, " 'Creation' and 'Creature'. 1. Some Texts and Tendencies," *Bij* 18 (1957): 129-39.

0126   A. Hockel, *Christus der Erstgeborene: Zur Geschichte der Exegese von Kol. 1, 15*. Düsseldorf: Patmos, 1965.

0127   T. F. Glasson, "Colossians 1,15-18 and Sirach 24," *JBL* 86 (1967): 214-16.

0128   André Feuillet, "Le Christ 'Premier-Né de toute créature' (Col 1,15) et la christolo gie cosmique de saint Paul," in *Christologre paulinienne et tradition biblique*. Paris: Desclée de Brouwer, 1973. Pp. 48-70.

1:15-17

0129   Robert M. Grant, "The Christ at the Creation," in R. Joseph Hoffmann and Gerald A Larue, eds., *Jesus in History and Myth*. Buffalo NY: Prometheus Books, 1986. Pp. 157-167.

1:15-16

    0130   David Schneider, "Colossians 1:15-16 and the Philippine Spirit World," *SEAJT* 15 (1974): 91-101.

1:15

    0131   G. W. H. Lampe, "New Testament Doctrine of *Ktisis*," *SJT* 17 (1964): 449-62.

    0132   R. Cantalamessa, "Cristo immagine di Dio. Le tradizioni patristiche su Col. 1,15," in *La Cristologia in san Paolo*. Brescia: Paideia, 1976. Pp. 269-87.

    0133   U. Vanni, "Immagine di Dio invisibile, primogenito di ogni creazione," in *La Cristologia in san Paolo*. Brescia: Paideia, 1976. Pp. 97-113.

    0134   T. Evan Pollard, "Exit the Alexandrian Christ: Some Reflections on Contemporary Christology in the Light of New Testament Studies," *CANZTR* 13 (1980): 16-23.

    0135   Hans H. Esser, "Zur Anthropologie Calvins: Menschenwürde--Imago Dei zwischen humanistischem und theologischem Ansatz," in Hans-Georg Geyer, et al., eds., *"Wenn nicht jetzt, wann dann"* (festschrift for Hans-Joachim Kraus). Neukirchen-Vluyn: Neukirchener Verlag, 1983. Pp. 269-81.

    0136   Jeffery Gibbs, "The Grace of God as the Foundation for Ethics," *CTQ* 48 (1984): 185-201.

    0137   Henri Crouzel, "Die Spiritualität des Origenes: Ihre Bedeutung für die Gegenwart," *TQ* 165 (1985): 132-42.

    0138   Rolf Gögler, "Inkarnationsglaube und Bibeltheologie bei Origenes," *TQ* 165 (1985): 82-94.

    0139   Paul Kalluveettil, "Prayer as Celebration: Towards the Merging of the Divine Human Milieus in the Bible," *JDharma* 10 (1985): 258-79.

    0140   Pol Vonck, "Imaging the Unimagible: Biblical Rootage of Art," *AFER* 27 (1985): 260-67.

    0141   Terence E. Fretheim, "The Color of God: Israel's God-Talk and Life Experience," *WW* 6 (1986): 256-65.

0142 Larry R. Helyer, "Arius Revisited: The Firstborn over All Creation," *JETS* 31 (1988): 59-67.

0143 David H. Johnson, "The Image of God in Colossians," *Did* 3 (1992): 9-15.

1:16-20
0144 John D. Laurence, "The Eucharist as the Imitation of Christ," *TS* 47 (1986): 286-96.

1:16
0145 André Feuillet, "La Création de l'Univers 'dans le Christ' d'après l'Épître aux Colossiens (i. 16a)," *NTS* 12 (1965-1966): 1-9.

0146 Pierre Benoit, "Pauline Angelology and Demonology: Reflexions on Designations of Heavenly Powers and on Origin of Angelic Evil according to Paul," *RSB* 3 (1983): 1-18.

0147 Walter Kasper, "Hope in the Final Coming of Jesus Christ in Glory," *CICR* 12 (1985): 368-84.

1:17-19
0148 David E. Garland, "First-Century Philosophers and Monotheism," *BI* 12/3 (1986): 16-19.

1:18
0149 P. Dacquino, "Cristo capo del corpo che è la chiesa," in *La Cristologia in san Paolo*. Brescia: Paideia, 1976. Pp. 131-75.

0150 Wayne Grudem, "Does *Kephale* ('Head') Mean 'Source' or 'Authority over' in Greek Literature: A Survey of 2,336 Examples," *TriJ* NS 6 (1985): 38-59.

0151 Bernhard Hanssler, "Autorität in der Kirche," *IKaZ* 14 (1985): 493-504.

1:19-33
0152 Traian Valdman, "Uno sguardo ortodosso sulla giustificazione in Lutero," *SEcu* 1 (1983): 277-88.

1:19-20
0153 Settimio Cipriani, "La croce di Cristo 'segno e fattore' di unità in Efesini e Colossesi," in Italo Mancini, et al., *La sapienza della croce*

oggi, 3: la sapienza della croce nella cultura e nella pastorale. Turin: Elle Di Ci, 1976. Pp. 553-67.

1:19

0154 Johannes L. Witte, "Die Katholizität der Kirche: eine neue Interpretation nach alter Tradition," *Greg* 42 (1961): 193-241.

0155 Gerhard Münderlein, "Die Erwählung durch das Pleroma--Kol 1:19," *NTS* 8 (1961-1962): 264-76.

0156 Hugolinus Langkammer, "Die Einwohnung der 'absoluten Seinsfülle' in Christus Bemerkungen zu Kol 1,19," *BZ* NS 12 (1968): 258-63.

0157 J. Ernst, "Kol 1, 19," in *Pleroma und Pleroma Christi Geschichte und Deutung eines Begriffs der paulinischen Antilegomena.* Regensburg: Pustet, 1970. Pp. 72-94.

0158 G. Bernini, "La pienezza di Cristo alla luce di alcuni testi veterotestamentari," in *La Cristologia in san Paolo.* Brescia: Paideia, 1976. Pp. 207-19.

0159 S. A. Panimolle, "L'inabitazione del plērōma nel Cristo," in *La Cristologia in san Paolo.* Brescia: Paideia, 1976. Pp. 177-205.

1:20-27
0160 Richard D. Patterson, "Peace, Part 2," *FundJ* 3 (1984): 59.

1:20
0161 Peter T. O'Brien, "Colossians 1:20 and the Reconciliation of All Things," *RTR* 33 (1974): 45-53.

0162 A. Sacchi, "La riconcil zione universale (Col. 1,20)," in *La Cristologia in san Paolo.* Brescia: Paideia, 1976. Pp. 221-45.

0163 Carmelo Granado Bellido, "Simbolismo del vestido: interpretación patrística de Gen 49:11," *EE* 59 (1984): 313-57.

1:21-23
0164 Robert A. Peterson, "The Perseverance of the Saints: A Theological Exegesis of Four Key New Testament Passages," *Pres* 17 (1991): 95-112.

1:21

0165 Henry J. Stob, "Natural Law Ethics: An Appraisal," *CTJ* 20 (1985): 58-68.

1:23

0166 Leopold Sabourin, "Paul and His Thought in Recent Research," *RSB* 2 (1982): 62-73; 3 (1983): 117-31.

0167 Eugene W. Bunkowske, "Was Luther a Missionary?" *CTQ* 49 (1985): 161-79.

0168 Jean Y. Thériault, "La femme chrétienne dans les textes pauliniens," *ScE* 37 (1985): 297-317.

1:24-29

0169 M. J. Kingston, "Suffering," *ET* 94 (1983): 144-45.

1:24-25

0170 Michael Cahill, "The Neglected Parallelism in Colossians 1:24-25," *ETL* 68 (1992): 142-47.

1:24

0171 P. Dacquino, "Al valore della sofferenza cristiana," *BibO* 8 (1906): 241-44.

0172 W. R. G. Moir, "Colossians 1,24," *ET* 42 (1930-1931): 479-80.

0173 J. Kremer, *Was an den Leiden Christi noch mangelt Eine interpretationsgeschichtliche und exegetische Untersuchung zu Kol. 1,24b*. BBB #12. Bonn: Hanstein, 1956.

0174 George H. P. Thompson, "Ephesians 3:13 and 2 Timothy 2:10 in the Light of Colossians 1:24," *ET* 71 (1960): 187-89.

0175 H. Gustafson, "The Afflictions of Christ: What is Lacking?" *BR* 8 (1963): 28-42.

0176 J. Blenkinsopp, "We Rejoice in Our Suffering," *Way* 7 (1967): 36-44.

0177 C. Lavergne, "La joie de saint Paul d'après Colossiens 1:24," *RT* 68 (1968): 419-34.

0178 Roy Yates, "Note on Colossians 1:24," *EQ* 42 (1970): 88-92.

0179   L. Paul Trudinger, "Further Brief Note on Colossians 1:24," *EQ* 45 (1973): 36-38.

0180   Richard J. Bauckham, "Colossians 1:24 Again: The Apocalyptic Motif," *EQ* 47 (1975): 168-70.

0181   S. Zedda, "La povertà di Cristo secondo S. Paolo," in *Evangelizare pauperibus*. Brescia: Paideia, 1978. Pp. 343-69.

0182   W. F. Flemington, "On the Interpretation of Colossians 1:24," in W. Horbury and B. McNeil, eds., *Suffering and Martyrdom in the New Testament* (festschrift for G. M. Styler). Cambridge: University Press, 1981. Pp. 84-90.

0183   Anthony Bloom, "What It Means to Be a Christian according to St. Paul," *JMosP* 6 (1983): 73-75.

0184   Gerhard Sauter, "Leiden und 'Handeln'," *EvT* 45 (1985): 435-58.

0185   Eduard Schweizer, "Askese nach Kol 1,24 oder 2,20f?" in Helmut Merklein, ed., *Neues Testament und Ethik* (festschrift for Rudolf Schnackenburg). Freiburg: Herder, 1989. Pp. 340-48.

0186   Andrew C. Perriman, "The Pattern of Christ's Sufferings: Colossians 1:24 and Philippians 3:10-11," *TynB* 42 (1991): 62-79.

0187   John H. P. Reumann, "How Do We Interpret 1 Timothy 2:1-5?" in H. George Anderson, et al., eds., *The One Mediator, the Saints, and Mary*. Minneapolis: Augsburg, 1992. Pp. 149-57.

1:25

0188   Carl Diemer, "Deacons and Other Endangered Species: A Look at the Biblical Office of Deacon," *FundJ* 3 (1984): 21-24.

1:26-2:3

0189   Galen W. Wiley, "A Study of 'Mystery' in the New Testament," *GTJ* 6 (1985): 349-60.

1:26-27

0190   R. Schnackenburg, "Das Christusgeheimnis (Kol 1,26-27)," in *Glaubensimpulse aus dem Neuen Testament*. Düsseldorf: Patmos, 1972. Pp. 123-27.

1:27-29

0191   Richard D. Patterson, "Laboring for Christ," *FundJ* 4 (1985): 67.

1:27

0192   W. P. Bowers, "A Note on Colossians 7a," in *Current Issues in Biblical and Patristic Interpretation* (festschrift for Merrill C. Tenney). Grand Rapids: Eerdmans, 1975. Pp. 110-14.

1:28-29

0193   Henry Ginder, "The Spirit's Empowerment in the Third Way," in Henry J. Schmidt, ed., *Witnesses of a Third Way: A Fresh Look at Evangelism*. Elgin IL: Brethren Press, 1986. Pp. 55-61.

1:28

0194   J. Leal, "Ut exhibeamus omnem hominem perfectum in Christo," *VD* 18 (1938): 178-86.

1:29-2:1

0195   V. C. Pfitzner, "Contending for the Faith - the Pale Alhletic Termini," in *Paul and the Agon Motif: Traditional Atheletic Imagery in the Pauline Literature*. Leiden: Brill, 1967. Pp. 109-29.

1:29

0196   Jean Y. Thériault, "La femme chrétienne dans les textes pauliniens," *ScE* 37 (1985): 297-317.

2:1

0197   E. Best, "Dead in Trespasses and Sins," *JSNT* 13 (1981): 9-25.

2:2-4

0198   A. J. Bandstra, "Did the Colossian Errorist Need a Mediator?" in R. N. Longenecker and M. C. Tenney, eds., *New Dimensions in New Testament Study*. Grand Rapids: Zondervan, 1974. Pp. 329-43.

2:2-3

0199   Pierre Benoit, "Colossiens 2:2-3," in William C. Weinrich, ed., *The New Testament Age* (festschrift for Bo Reicke). 2 vols. Macon GA: Mercer Universitry Press, 1984. 1:41-51.

2:6-23

0200   J. Lähnemann, "Die Exegese von Kolosser 2,6-23," in *Der Kolosserbrief*. Gütersloh: G. Mohn, 1971. Pp. 110-52.

0201   H. Halter, "Kol 2,6-23. Begraben und auferweckt mit Christus, befreit von Sündentod und kosmischem Mächten," in *Taufe und Ethos: Paulinische Kriterien für das Proprium christlicher Moral*. Freiburg: Herder, 1977. Pp. 190-203.

2:6-19

0202   Holly D. Hayes, "Colossians 2:6-19," *Int* 49 (1995): 285-88.

2:6-15

0203   Jean Perret, "Notes bibliques de prédication sur trois péricopes de l'Épître de saint Paul aux Colossiens," *VerbC* 19 (1965): 57-64.

0204   Roy A. Harrisville, "God's Mercy - Tested, Promised, Done! An Exposition of Genesis 18:20-32; Luke 11:1-13; Colossians 2:6-15," *Int* 31 (1977): 165-78.

0205   J. O'Neill, "The Source of Christology in Colossians," *NTS* 26 (1979-1980): 87-100.

0206   Robert Paul Roth, "Christ and the Powers of Darkness: Lessons from Colossians," *WW* 6 (1986): 336-44.

2:6-7

0207   Otto Merk, "Erwägungen zu Kol 2,6f," in Hubert Frankemölle and Karl Kertelge, eds., *Vom Urchristentum zu Jesus* (festschrift for Joachim Gnilka). Freiburgi: Herder, 1989. Pp. 407-16.

2:7

0208   P. M. Tapernoux, *Enracines et Edifies en Lui* Vevey: Editions Bible et Traites Chretiens, 1964.

2:8-3:4

0209   Henry I. Lederle, "Better the Devil You Know: Seeking a Biblical Basis for the Societal Dimension of Evil and/or the Demonic in the Pauline Concept of the 'Powers'," in Pieter G. R. De Villiers, ed., *Like a Roaring Lion: Essays on the Bible, the Church and Demonic Powers*. Pretoria: University of South Africa, 1987. Pp. 102-20.

2:8-23

0210   L. Vogel, *Die Philosophie (Kol. 2, 8-23): und das Wort Gottes (Offbg. 19, 13)*. Zurich: Vogel-Verlag, 1960.

2:8-20

0211 J. Huby, "*Stoikeia* dans Bardesane et saint Paul," *Bib* 15 (1934): 365-68.

2:8-15

0212 C. S. Rodd, "Salvation Proclaimed. XI. Colossians 28-15," *ET* 94 (1982): 36-41.

2:8-10

0213 G. Bornkamm, "Die Häresie des Kolosserbriefes," *TLZ* 73 (1948): 11-20.

0214 Eduard Schweizer, "Die Elemente der Welt Gal 4,3.9, Kol 2,8.20," in *Festschiift für G Stählin*. Wuppertal: R. Brockhaus, 1970. Pp. 245-59.

2:8

0215 Joe B. McMinn, "An Historical Treatment of the Greek Phrase τὰ στοιχεῖα (Galatians 4:3 and Colossians 2:8, 20)," doctoral dissertation, Southern Baptist Theological Seminary, Louisville KY, 1950.

0216 Willis Dulap, "Two Fragments: Theological Transformation of Law, Technological Transformation of Nature," in Carl Mitcham and Jim Grote, eds., *Theology and Technology: Essays in Christian Analysis and Exegesis*. Lanham MD: University Press of America, 1984. Pp. 227-35.

0217 Eduard Schweizer, "Slaves of the Elements and Worshipers of Angels," *JBL* 107 (1988): 455-68.

0218 Michelangelo Tabet, "I testi paolini sulla paradosis nei commenti patristici," in Willy Rordorf, et al., eds., *La tradizione: forme e modi: XVIII Incontro di studiosi dell'antichità cristiana*. Rome: Institutum Patristicum Augustinianum, 1990. Pp. 39-53.

0219 Dietrich Rusam, "Neue Belege zu den stoicheia tou kosmou," *ZNW* 83 (1992): 119-25.

2:9-15

0220 G. Schille, "Kolosser 2, 9-15,"in *Frühchristliche Hymnen*. Berlin: Evangelische Verlagsanstalt, 1965. Pp. 31-37.

2:9-10

0221   J. Ernst, "Kol 2,9f.," in *Pleroma und Pleroma Christi: Geschichte und Deutung eines Begriffs der paulinischen Antilegomena.* Regensburg: Pustet, 1970. Pp. 94-105.

2:9

0222   Anton Anwander, "Zu Kol 2:9," *BZ* NS 9 (1965): 278-80.

0223   Lars Hartman, "Kroppsligen, 'personligen' eller vad? Till Kol 2:9," *SEÅ* 51-52 (1986): Pp. 72-79.

2:10

0224   Pierre Benoit, "Pauline Angelology and Demonology: Reflexions on Designations of Heavenly Powers and on Origin of Angelic Evil according to Paul," *RSB* 3 (1983): 1-18.

0225   Wayne Grudem, "Does *Kephale* ('Head') Mean 'Source' or 'Authority over' in Greek Literature: A Survey of 2,336 Examples," *TriJ* NS 6 (1985): 38-59.

2:11-3:4

0226   E. Larsson, *Christus als Vorbild: Eine Untersuchung zu den paulinischen Tauf- und Eikontexten.* Uppsala: Almquist & Wiksells, 1962. Pp. 80-92.

2:11-15

0227   0. Kuss, "Zur paulinischen und nachpaulinischen Tauflehre," *TGl* 42 (1952): 401-25.

2:11-13

0228   G. Sellin, " 'Die Auferstehung ist schon geschehen'. Zur Spiritualsierung apokalyptischer Terminologie im Neuen Testament," *NovT* 25 (1983): 220-37.

0229   Kenneth Grayston, "The Opponents in Philippians 3," *ET* 97 6 (1986): 170-72.

2:11-12

0230   Robert A. Coughenour, "Fullness of Life in Christ: Exegetical Study on Colossians 2:11-12," *RR* 31 (1977): 52-56.

0231   Paul D. Gardner, "Circumcised in Baptism - Raised through Faith: A Note on Colossians 2:11-12," *WTJ* 45 (1983): 172-77.

2:11

0232   M. Van Esbroeck, "Col 2,11 'Dans la circoncision du Christ'," in J. Ries and J.-M. Sevrin, eds., *Gnosticisme et monde hellénistique.* Louvain: Institut Orientaliste, 1980. Pp. 68-70.

0233   Lynn Jones, "Circumcision Among Jews of the Dispersion," *BI* 12/3 (1986): 24-27.

0234   Evertt Ferguson, "Spiritual Circumcision in Early Christinaity," *SJT* 41 (1988): 485-97.

2:12-14

0235   C. Bigaré, "La croix, source de vie (Col 2)," *AsSeign* NS 48 (1972): 55-60.

2:12

0236   Harold H. Buls, "Luther's Translation of Colossians 2:12," *CTQ* 45 (1981): 13-16.

0237   Harold L. Willmington, "The Spirit of God and the Saints of God," *FundJ* 2 (1983): 43-44.

0238   Gerard S. Sloyan, "Jewish Ritual of the 1st century CE and Christian Sacramental Behavior," *BTB* 15 (1985): 98-103.

2:13-15

0239   Eduard Lohse, "Ein hymnisches Bekenntnis in Kol 2,13-15," in A.-L. Descamps and André Halleux, eds., *Mélanges bibliques en hommage au R. P. Béda Rigaux.* Gembloux: Duculot, 1970. Pp. 427-35.

0240   Klaus Wengst, "Das Versöhnungslied," in *Christologische Formeln and Lieder des Ur christentums.* Gütersloh: G. Mohn, 1972. Pp. 181-94.

0241   Stanley J. Samartha, "Religion, Culture and Power - Three Bible Studies," *RS* 34 (1987): 66-79.

2:13

0242   William L. Craig, "The Historicity of the Empty Tomb of Jesus," *NTS* 31 (1985): 39-67.

2:14-15

0243   Aidan Breen, "The Liturgical Materials in MS Oxford, Bodleian Library, Auct F4/32," *AL* 34 (1992): 121-53.

0244 Rudolf Hoppe, "Theologie in den Deuteropaulinen," in Hans J. Klauck, ed., *Monotheismus und Christologie: zur Gottesfrage im hellenistischen Judentum und im Urchristentum.* Freiburg: Herder, 1992. Pp. 163-86.

0245 A. T. Hanson, "The Conquest of the Powers," in *Studies in Paul's Technique and Theology.* London: SPCK, 1974. Pp. 1-12.

2:14

0246 A. Vallisoleto, "Delens chirographum," *VD* 12 (1932): 181-85.

0247 O. A. Blanchette, "Does the χειρόγραφον of Colossians 2:14 Represent Christ Himself," *CBQ* 23 (1961): 306-12.

0248 Wesley Carr, "Two Notes on Colossians," *JTS* 24 (1973): 492-500.

0249 N. Walter, "Die 'Handschrift in Satzungen' Kol 2,14," *ZNW* 70 (1979): 115-18.

0250 Roy Yates, "Colossians and Gnosis," *JSNT* 27 (1986): 49-68.

0251 Roy Yates, "Colossians 2,14: Metaphor of Forgiveness," *Bib* 71/2 (1990): 248-59.

2:15

0252 A. Vallisoleto, "Et spolian principatus et potestates," *VD* 13 (1933): 187-92.

0253 Lamar Williamson, "Led in Triumph: Paul's Use of *Thriambeuo*," *Int* 22 (1968): 317-32.

0254 R. B. Egan, "Lexical Evidence on Two Pauline Passages," *NovT* 19 (1977): 34-62.

0255 Pierre Benoit, "Pauline Angelology and Demonology: Reflexions on Designations of Heavenly Powers and on Origin of Angelic Evil according to Paul," *RSB* 3 (1983): 1-18.

0256 Colin Gunton, "Christus Victor Revisited: A Study in Metaphor and the Transformation of Meaning," *JTS* NS 36 (1985): 129-45.

0257 Roy Yates, "Colossians 2:15: Christ Triumphant," *NTS* 37 (1991): 573-91.

0258 Darrell L. Bock, " 'The New Man' as Community in Colossians and Ephesians," in Charles H. Dyer and Roy B. Zuck, eds., *Integrity of Heart, Skillfulness of Hands: biblical and Leadership Studies* (festschrift for Donald K. Campbell. Grand Rapids: Baker Book House, 1994. Pp. 157-67.

2:16-3:17

0259 Gregory T. Christopher, "A Discourse Analysis of Colossians 2:16-3:17," *GTJ* 11 (1990): 205-20.

2:16-23

0260 W. Stephen Sabom, "The Gnostic World of Anorexia Nervosa," *JPT* 13 (1985): 243-54.

2:16-17

0261 Kenneth H. Wood, "The 'Sabbath Days' of Colossians 2:16,17," in Kenneth A. Strand, ed., *The Sabbath in Scripture and History.* Washington: Review and Herald Publication Association, 1982. Pp. 338-42.

2:16

0262 Paul Giem, "σαββάτων in Colossians 2:16," *AUSS* 19 (1981): 195-210.

0263 Timothy G. C. Thornton, "Jewish New Moon Festivals, Galatians 4:3-11 and Colossians 2:16," *JTS* NS 40 (1989): 97-100.

0264 Troy Martin, "Pagan and Judeo-Christian Time-Keeping Schemes in Galatians 4:10 and Colossians 2:16," *NTS* 42 (1996): 105-19.

2:17

0265 Troy Martin, "But Let Everyone Discern the Body of Christ," *JBL* 114 (1995): 249-55.

2:17-18

0266 I. A. Moir, "Some Thoughts on Col. 2,17-18," *TZ* 35 (1979): 363-65.

2:18

0267 Fred O. Francis, "Humility and Angelic Worship in Colossians 2:18," *StTheol* 16 (1962): 109-34.

0268 Stanislas Lyonnet, "L'Épître aux Colossiens (Col 2:18) et les mystères d'Apollon Clarien," *Bib* 43 (1962): 417-35.

0269   Wesley Carr, "Two Notes on Colossians," *JTS* 24 (1973): 492-500.

0270   Roy Yates, "The Worship of Angels," *ET* 97 (1985): 12-15.

0271   Eduard Schweizer, "Slaves of the Elements and Worshipers of Angels," *JBL* 107 (1988): 455-68.

0272   Michael D. Goulder, "Vision and Knowledge," *JSNT* 56 (1994): 53-71.

2:19

0273   S. Tromp, "aput influit sensum et mortum," *Greg* 39 (1958): 353-66.

0274   Wayne Grudem, "Does *Kephale* ('Head') Mean 'Source' or 'Authority over' in Greek Literature: A Survey of 2,336 Examples," *TriJ* NS 6 (1985): 38-59.

2:20-3:4

0275   J. P. Louw, "Reading a Text as Discourse," in David A. Black, et al., eds., *Linguistics and New Testament Interpretation: Essays on Discourse Analysis*. Nashville: Broadman Press, 1992. Pp. 17-30.

2:20-21

0276   Eduard Schweizer, "Askese nach Kol 1,24 oder 2,20f?" in Helmut Merklein, ed., *Neues Testament und Ethik* (festschrift for Rudolf Schnackenburg). Freiburg: Herder, 1989. Pp. 340-48.

2:20

0277   Joe B. McMinn, "An Historical Treatment of the Greek Phrase τὰ στοιχεῖα (Galatians 4:3 and Colossians 2:8, 20)," doctoral dissertation, Southern Baptist Theological Seminary, Louisville KY, 1950.

0278   Eduard Schweizer, "Die Elemente der Welt Gal 4, 3. 9; Kol 2, 8. 20," in O. Böcher and K. Haacker, eds., *Verborum Veritas* (festschrift for Gustav Stählin). Wuppertal: Brockhaus, 1970. Pp. 245-59.

0279   Willis Dulap, "Two Fragments: Theological Transformation of Law, Technological Transformation of Nature," in Carl Mitcham and Jim Grote, eds., *Theology and Technology: Essays in Christian Analysis and Exegesis*. Lanham MD: University Press of America, 1984. Pp. 227-35.

0280   Eduard Schweizer, "Slaves of the Elements and Worshipers of Angels," *JBL* 107 (1988): 455-68.

0281   Eduard Schweizer, "Altes und Neues zu den 'Elementen der Welt' in Kol 2,20; Gal 4,3-9," in Kurt Aland and Siegfried Meurer, eds., - *Wissenschaft und Kirche* (festschrift for Eduard Lohse). Bielefeld: Luther-Verlag, 1989. Pp. 111-18.

0282   Dietrich Rusam, "Neue Belege zu den stoicheia tou kosmou," *ZNW* 83 (1992): 119-25.

2:23

0283   B. Reicke, "Zum sprachlichen Verständnis von Kol. 2,23," *StTheol* 6 (1953): 39-53.

0284   Bernhard Hanssler, "Zu Satzkonstruktion und Aussage in Kol 2,23," in H. Feld and J. Nolte, eds., *Wort Gottes in der Zeit* (festschrift for Karl H. Schelkle). Düsseldorf: Patmos, 1973. Pp. 143-48.

0285   B. Hollenbach, "Col. 2.23: Which Things Lead to the Fulfilment of the Flesh," *NTS* 25 (1978-1979): 254-61.

3:1-4:6

0286   Peter T. O'Brien, "The Church as a Heavenly and Eschatological Entity," in Don A. Carson, ed., *The Church in the Bible and the World: An International Study.* Exeter: Paternoster Press, 1987. Pp. 88-119.

0287   Roy Yates, "The Christian Way of Life: The Paraenetic Material in Colossians 3:1-4:6," *EQ* 63 (1991): 241-51.

3:1-17

0288   C. F. D. Moule, "New Life in Colossians 3:1-17," *RevExp* 70 (1973): 481-93.

0289   H. Merklein, "Eph 4,1-5,20 als Rezeption von Kol 3,1-17 (zugleich ein Beitrag zur Problematik des Epheserbriefes)," in P.-G. Müller and W. Stenger, eds., *Kontinuität und Einheit* (festschrift for Franz Mussner). Freiburg: Herder, 1981. Pp. 194-210.

3:1-15

0290   Jean Perret, "Notes bibliques de prédication sur trois péricopes de l'Épître de saint Paul aux Colossiens," *VerbC* 19 (1965): 57-64.

3:1-11

0291   M. Trimaille, "Mort et résurrection dans la vie des baptisés (Col 3),"
        AsSeign NS 49 (1971): 72-81.

3:1-8

0292   G. Crespy, "Col. 3:1-8," *ETR* 30 (1955): 76-79.

3:1-6

0293   John R. Levison, "2 Apoc Bar 48:42-52:7 and the Apocalyptic
        Dimension of Colossians 3:1-6," *JBL* 108 (1989): 93-108.

3:1-4

0294   T. Camelot, "Ressuscités avec le Christ," *VS* 84 (1951): 354-63.

0295   Erich Grässer, "Kol 3, 1-4 als Beispiel einer Interpretation secundum
        homines recipientes," *ZTK* 64 (1967): 139-68.

0296   G. Gaide, "Le Christ, votre vie," *AsSeign* 21 (1969): 84-89.

0297   H. Halter, "Kol 3,1-4. Gestorben und erweckt mit Christus: suchet
        was 'oben' ist!" in *Taufe und Ethos: Paulinische Kriterien für das
        Proprium christlicher Moral*. Freiburg: Herder, 1977. Pp. 204-209.

0298   A. Viard, "Une vie nouvelle avec le Christ (Col.3,1-4)," *EV* 78
        (1978): 59-60.

0299   A. del Pérez Agua, "Derás cristológico del Salmo 110 en el Neuvo
        Testamento," in Marcos Fernández, et al., eds., *Simposio Biblico
        Español*. Madrid: Universidad Complutense, 1984. Pp. 637-62.

0300   Edouard Delebecque, "Sur un problème de temps chez Saint Paul," -
        Bib 70 (1989): 389-95.

3:1-3

0301   John E. Booty, "Christian Spirituality: From Wilberforce to Temple
        (Colossians 3:1-3)," in William J. Wolf, ed., *Angican Spirituality*.
        Wilton CN: Morehouse-Barlow, 1982. Pp. 69-103.

3:1

0302   F. Wulf, "Suchet, was droben ist, wo Christus ist, sitzend sur Rechten
        Gottes," *GeistL* 41 (1968): 161-64.

0303 Michel Gourgues, "Colossiens 3:1," in *la droite de Dieu: Résurrection de Jésus et actualisation du Psaume 110:1 dans le Nouveau Testament*. Paris: Gabalda, 1978. Pp. 57-63.

0304 Romano Penna, "Dialettica tra ricerca e scoperta di Dio nell'epistolario paolino," in Nicolò M. Loss et al., eds., *Quaerere Deum: Atti della XXV Settimana Biblica*. Brescia: Paideia Editrice, 1980. Pp. 315-51.

0305 Traian Valdman, "Uno sguardo ortodosso sulla giustificazione in Lutero," *SEcu* 1 (1983): 277-88.

0306 David H. C. Read, "Gentle Jesus or Cosmic Christ," *ET* 96 (1985): 213-14.

3:2-4

0307 Robert Leuenberger, "Was droben ist," *Reformatio* 21 (1972): 202-206.

3:3-4

0308 R. Schnackenburg, "Verborgene Herrlichkeit (Kol 3,34)," in *Glaubensimpulse aus dem Neuen Testament*. Düsseldorf: Patmos, 1972. Pp. 128-32.

3:3

0309 Leopold Sabourin, "Paul and His Thought in Recent Research," *RSB* 2 (1982): 62-73; 3 (1983): 117-31.

0310 Luis F. Ladaria, "Presente y futuro en la escatología cristiana," *EE* 60 (1985): 351-59.

3:5-17

0311 H. Halter, "Kol 3,5-17. Der alte Mensch ist abgetan, ein neuer ist geworden: zieht den alten aus und den neuen an!" in *Taufe und Ethos: Paulinische Kriterien für das Proprium christlicher Moral*. Freiburg: Herder, 1977. Pp. 209-26.

3:5-15

0312 B. Rey, "L'homme nouveau d'après S. Paul," *RSPT* 48 (1964): 603-629; 49 (1965): 161-95.

0313 B. Rey, "L'existence pascale di baptisé: Lecture de Colossiens 3:5-15," *VS* 113 (1967): 696-718.

3:5-11

0314   P. Joüon, "Note sur Col 3,5-11," *RechSR* 26 (1936): 185-89.

3:6-4:1

0315   Lars Hartman, "Code and Context: A Few Reflections on the Parenesis of Colossians 3:6-4:1," in Gerald F. Hawthorne and Otto Betz, eds., *Tradition and Interpretation in the New Testament* (festschrift for E. Earle Ellis). Grand Rapids MI: Eerdmans, 1987. Pp. 237-47.

3:9-11

0316   J. Jervell, "Gen 1,26f. in der Taufparänese," in *Imago Dei: Gen 1.26f im Spätjudentum, in der Gnosis und in den paulinischen Briefen.* FRLANT #76. Göttingen: Vandenhoeck & Ruprecht, 1960. Pp. 231-56.

0317   Kenneth Grayston, "The Opponents in Philippians 3," *ET* 97 6 (1986): 170-72.

3:9

0318   Stanley E. Porter, "P Oxy 744.4 and Colossians 3:9," *Bib* 73 (1992): 565-67.

3:10-12

0319   E. Larsson, *Christus als Vorbild: Eine Untersuchung zu den paulinischen Tauf- und Eikontexten.* Uppsala: Almquist & Wiksells, 1962. Pp. 188-223.

3:10-11

0320   Michel Bouttier, "Complexio Oppositorum: sur les Formules de 1 Cor. xii. 13; Gal. iii.26-8; Col. iii. 10, 11," *NTS* 23 (1976-1977): 1-19.

3:10

0321   Hans H. Esser, "Zur Anthropologie Calvins: Menschenwürde--Imago Dei zwischen humanistischem und theologischem Ansatz," in Hans-Georg Geyer, et al., eds., *"Wenn nicht jetzt, wann dann"* (festschrift for Hans-Joachim Kraus). Neukirchen-Vluyn: Neukirchener Verlag, 1983. Pp. 269-81.

0322   Willis Dulap, "Two Fragments: Theological Transformation of Law, Technological Transformation of Nature," in Carl Mitcham and Jim Grote, eds., *Theology and Technology: Essays in Christian Analysis* *and Exegesis*. Lanham MD: University Press of America, 1984. Pp. 227-35.

0323   Jeffery Gibbs, "The Grace of God as the Foundation for Ethics," *CTQ* 48 (1984): 185-201.

0324   LeRoy S. Capper, "The Imago Dei and Its Implications for Order in the Church," *Pres* 11 (1985): 21-33.

0325   Mikeal Parsons, "The New Creation," *ET* 99 (1987): 3-4.

0326   David H. Johnson, "The Image of God in Colossians," *Did* 3 (1992): 9-15.

3:11

0327   Walter H. Principe, "The Dignity and Rights of the Human Person as Saved, as Being Saved, as to Be Saved by Christ," *Greg* 65 (1984): 389-430.

0328   Mikeal Parsons, "Slavery and the New Testament: Equality and Submissiveness," *VoxE* 18 (1988): 89-96.

0329   Troy Martin, "The Scythian Perspective in Colossians 3:11," *NovT* 37 (1995): 249-61.

0330   Douglas A. Campbell, "Unravelling Colossians 3:11b," *NTS* 42 (1996): 120-32.

0331   Douglas A. Campbell, "The Scythian Perspective in Colossians 3:11: A Response to Troy Martin," *NovT* 39 (1997): 81-84.

3:12-21

0332   C. Bigaré, "Amour et union dans le Seigneur (Col 3)," *AsSeign* NS 11 (1971): 13-18.

0333   A. Viard, "Famille et vie chrétienne (Col. 3,12-2 1)," *EV* 78 (1978): 329-30; 82 (1982) 358-59.

3:12-17

0334   F. Ogara, "Caritatem habete, quod est vinculum perfecrionis," *VD* 17 (1937): 335-43.

0335 T. Maertens, "Amiez-vous dans le Seigneur," *AsSeign* 14 (1961): 13-24.

0336 H. J. Spital, "Christliches Leben ist Leben aus der Freude. Eine Homilie über Kol 3,12-17," *BibL* 2 (1961): 53-59.

3:12-14

0337 Richard D. Patterson, "Christian Patience," *FundJ* 3 (1984): 55.

0338 Joseph Allen, "Renewal of the Christian Community: A Challenge for the Pastoral Ministry," *SVTQ* 29 (1985): 305-23.

3:12

0339 Klaus Wengst, "Einander durch Demut für vorzüglicher zu halten: Zum Begriff 'Demut' bei Paulus und in paulinischer Tradition," in Wolfgang Schrage, ed., *Studien zum Text und zur Ethik des Neuen Testaments* (festschrift for Heinrich Greeven). Berlin: Walter de Gruyter, 1986. Pp. 428-39.

3:14

0340 W. Stephen Sabom, "The Gnostic World of Anorexia Nervosa," *JPT* 13 (1985): 243-54.

3:16-4:1

0341 William Lillie, "Pauline House-Tables," *ET* 86 (1975): 179-83.

3:16-17

0342 Austin C. Lovelace, "Make a Joyful Noise to the Lord: Biblical Foundations of Church Music," *Point* 2 (1973): 15-27.

3:17

0343 Traian Valdman, "Uno sguardo ortodosso sulla giustificazione in Lutero," *SEcu* 1 (1983): 277-88.

3:18-4:1

0344 Winsome Munro, "Colossians 3:18-4:1 and Ephesians 5:21-6:9: Evidences of a Late Literary Stratum?" *NTS* 18 (1971-1972): 434-47.

0345 L. Goppelt, "Jesus und die 'Haustafel' Tradition," in *Orientierung an Jesus: Zur Theologie der Synoptiker* (festschrift for Josef Schmid). Freiburg: Herder, 1973. Pp. 93-106.

0346   E. Glenn Hinson, "Christian Household in Colossians 3:18-4:1," *RevExp* 70 (1973): 495-506.

0347   K. Thraede, "Zum historischen Hintergrund der 'Haustafeln' des NT," in E. Dassmann, ed., *Pietas* (festschrift for Bernhard Kötting). Münster: Westfalen, 1980, Pp. 359-68.

0348   William R. Herzog, "The 'Household Duties' Passages: Apostolic Traditions and Contemporary Concerns," *Found* 24 (1981): 204-15.

0349   Karlheinz Müller, "Die Haustafel des Kolosserbriefes und das antike Frauenthema: Eine kritische Rückschau auf alte Ergebnisse," in Gerhard Dautzenberg, et al., eds., *Die Frau im Urchristentum*. Freiburg: Herder, 1983. Pp. 263-319.

0350   Frank Stagg, "The Gospel, Haustafel, and Women: Mark 1:1; Colossians 3:18-4:1," *FM* 2 (1985): 59-63.

0351   Robert L. Richardson, "From 'Subjection to Authority' to 'Mutual Submission': The Ethic of Subordination in 1 Peter," *FM* 4 (1987): 70-80.

0352   Lars Hartman, "Some Unorthodox Thoughts on the 'Household-Code Form'," in Jacob Neusner, et al., eds., *The Social World of Formative Christianity and Judaism* (festschrift for Howard Clark Kee). Philadelphia: Fortress Press, 1988. Pp. 219-32.

0353   Stephen Motyer, "The Relationship between Paul's Gospel of 'All One in Christ Jesus' (Galatians 3:28) and the 'Household Codes'," - *VoxE* 19 (1989): 33-48.

0354   R. Scott Nash, "Heuristic Haustafeln: Domestic Codes as Entrance to the Social World of Early Christianity: The Case of Colossians," in Jacob Neusner, et al., eds., *Religious Writings and Religious Systems: Systemic Analysis of Holy Books*. Volume 2. *Christianity*. Atlanta: Scholars Press, 1989. Pp. 25-50.

0355   Georg Strecker, "Die neutestamentlichen Haustafeln (Kol 3,18-4,1 und Eph 5,22-6,9)," in Helmut Merklein, ed., *Neues Testament und Ethik* (festschrift for Rudolf Schnackenburg). Freiburg: Herder, 1989. Pp. 349-75.

34 BIBLIOGRAPHIES FOR BIBLICAL RESEARCH

3:18-19

0356 H. Baltensweiler, "Kolosserbrief (Kap. 3, 18-19)," in *Die Ehe im Neuen Testament*. Stuttgart: Zwingle, 1967. Pp. 210-17.

0357 Orsay Groupe, "Une lecture féministe des 'codes domestiques'," *FV* 88 (1989): 59-69.

0358 George W. Knight, "Husbands and Wives as Analogues of Christ and the Church: Ephesians 5:21-33 and Colossians 3:18-19," in John Piper and Wayne A. Grudem, eds., *Recovering Biblical Manhood and Womanhood: A Response to Evangelical Feminism*. Wheaton: Crossway Books, 1991. Pp. 165-78; 492-95.

3:18

0359 Claus Bussmann, "Gibt es christologische Begründungen für eine Unterordnung der Frau im Neuen Testament?" in Gerhard Dautzenberg, et al., eds., *Die Frau im Urchristentum*. Freiburg: Herder, 1983. Pp. 254-62.

3:22

0360 Fred Catherwood, "The Protestant Work Ethic: Attitude and Application Give it Meaning," *FundJ* 2 (1983): 22-25.

4:2

0361 Evald Lövestram, "Ephesians 6:18, Colossians 4:2, etc.: Wakefulness and Prayer," in *Spiritual Wakefulness in the New Testament*. Lund: Gleerup, 1963. Pp. 64-77.

4:3-4

0362 Gene R. Smillie, "Ephesians 6:19-20: A Mystery for the Sake of Which the Apostle is an Ambassador in Chains," *TriJ* 18 (1997): 199-222.

4:3

0363 Markus N. A. Bockmuehl, "A Note on the Text of Colossians 4:3," *JTS* NS 39 (1988): 489-94.

4:5

0364 W. D. Thomas, "Luke, the Beloved Physician (Col 4,5)," *ET* 95 (1983-1984): 279-81.

4:6

0365 Urban C. Von Wahlde, "Mark 9:33-50: Discipleship: The Authority that Serves," *BZ* NS 29 (1985): 49-67.

4:7-18

0366 Eduard Lohse, "Die Mitarbeiter des Apostels Paulus im Kolosserbrief," in O. Böcher and K. Haacker, eds., *Verborum Veritas* (festschrift for Gustav Stählin). Wuppertal: Brockhaus, 1970. Pp. 189-94.

4:7-17

0367 Lamar Cope, "On Rethinking the Philemon-Colossians Connection," *BR* 30 (1985): 45-50.

0368 Bonnie Thurston, "Paul's Associates in Colossians 4:7-17," *RQ* 41 (1999): 45-55.

0369 George E. Ladd, "Paul's Friends in Colossians 4:7-16," *RevExp* 70 (1973): 507-14.

4:7

0370 Beverly R. Gaventa, "In Memory of Her: A Review Article," *LTQ* 20 (1985): 58-60.

4:10-11

0371 George Johnston, "Kingdom of God Sayings in Paul's Letters," in Peter Richardson and John C. Hurd, eds., *From Jesus to Paul* (festschrift for Francis W. Beare). Waterloo: Wilfrid Laurier University Press, 1984. Pp. 143-56.

4:10

0372 James A. Brooks, "Barnabas: All We Know," *BI* 12/3 (1986): 58-61.

0373 Rice A. Pierce, "Mark: All We Know," *BI* 12/3 (1986): 54-57.

4:11

0374 E. E. Ellis, " 'Those of the Circumcision' and the Early Christian Mission," *StudE* 4 (1968): 390-99.

4:12-13

0375 D. Edmond Hiebert, "Epaphras, Man of Prayer," *BSac* 136 (1979): 54-64.

4:14

0376 H. Evans, "Luke - the Good Companion," *ET* 91 (1980): 372-74.

4:15

0377   Ernst Dassmann, "Hausgemeinde und Bischofsamt," in Ernst
Dassmann and Klaus Thraede, eds., *Vivarium* (festschrift for Theodor
Klauser). Münster, West Germany: Aschendorff, 1984. Pp. 82-97.

0378   Marlis Giele, "Zur Interpretation der paulinischen Formel τὴν κατ᾽
οἶκον αὐτῆς ἐκκλησίαν," *ZNW* 77 (1986): 109-25.

4:16

0379   C. P. Anderson, "Who Wrote 'The Epistle from Laodicea'?" *JBL* 85
(1966): 436-40.

PART TWO

Citations by Subjects

angels

0380 John R. Levison, "2 Apoc Bar 48:42-52:7 and the Apocalyptic Dimension of Colossians 3:1-6," *JBL* 108 (1989): 93-108.

anthropology

0381 G. W. H. Lampe, "New Testament Doctrine of *Ktisis*," *SJT* 17 (1964): 449-62.

0382 Erich Grässer, "Kol 3, 1-4 als Beispiel einer Interpretation secundum homines recipientes," *ZTK* 64 (1967): 139-68.

0383 Lars Hartman, "Kroppsligen, 'personligen' eller vad? Till Kol 2:9," *SEÅ* 51-52 (1986): Pp. 72-79.

anthropomorphism

0384 Gedaliahu A. G. Stroumsa, "Form(s) of God: Some Notes on *Metatron* and Christ," *HTR* 76 (1983): 269-88.

antisemticism

0385 James D. G. Dunn, "Anti-Semitism in the Deutero-Pauline Literature," in Michael H. Barnes, eds., *An Ecology of the Spirit: Religious Reflection and Environmental Consciousness*. Lanham MD: University Press of America, 1994. Pp. 151-65.

apocalyptic literature

0386 Christopher Rowland, "Apocalyptic Visions and the Exaltation of Christ in the Letter to the Colossians," *JSNT* 19 (1983): 73-83.

0387 Randal A. Argall, "The Source of a Religious Error in Colossae," *CTJ* 22 (1987): 6-20.

0388 Andrew Chester, "Jewish Messianic Expectations and Mediatorial Figures and Pauline Christology," in Martin Hengel and Ulrich Heckel, eds., *Paulus und das antike Judentum* (festschriftr for Adolf Schlatter). Tübingen: Mohr, 1991. Pp. 17-89.

0389 Thomas J. Sappington, *Revelation and Redemption at Colossae*. Sheffield: JSOT Press, 1991.

atonement

0390 Ted Peters, "Atonement," *Dialog* 35 (1996): 7-41.

baptism
0391   E. Käsemann, "Eine urchristliche Taufliturgie," in *Exegetische Versuche und Besinnungen*. Göttingen: Vandenhoech & Ruprecht, 1965. 34-51.

0392   George R. Beasley-Murray, "Second Chapter of Colossians," *RevExp* 70 (1973): 469-79.

0393   Paul D. Gardner, "Circumcised in Baptism - Raised through Faith: A Note on Colossians 2:11-12," *WTJ* 45 (1983): 172-77.

0394   Vigen Guroian, "Seeing Worship as Ethics: An Orthodox Perspective," *JRE* 13 (1985): 332-59.

0395   Harold W. Attridge, "On Becoming an Angel: Nag Hammadi Rival Baptismal Theologies at Colossae," in Lukas Bormann, et al., eds., - *Religious Propaganda and Missionary Competition in the New Testament World* (feschrift for Dieter Georgi. Leiden: E. J. Brill, 1994. Pp. 481-98.

chiasmus
0396   Alfred E. Drake, "The Riddle of Colossians: Quaerendo invenietis," *NTS* 41 (1995): 123-44.

0397   John Behr, "Colossians 1:13-20: A Chiastic Reading," *SVTQ* 40 (1996): 247-64.

christology
0398   Matthias Slavic, *Des Ephesier - und Kolosser-briefes: Lehre über die Person Christi und sein Heilswerk*. Vienna: Mayer & Comp, 1911.

0399   Ralph M. Smith, "An Inquiry into the Nature of the Person and Work of Christ as Revealed in the Imprisonment Epistles," doctoral dissertation, Southwestern Baptist Theological Seminary, Fort Worth TX, 1960.

0400   O. A. Blanchette, "Does the χειρόγραφον of Colossians 2:14 Represent Christ Himself," *CBQ* 23 (1961): 306-12.

0401   James H. Burtness, "All the Fulness," *Dia* 3 (1964): 257-63.

0402   Kurt Scharf, "Scope of the Redemptive Task, Colossians 1:15-20," *CTM* 36 (1965): 291-300.

0403 Fred B. Craddock, "All Things in Him—A Critical Note on Colossians 1:15-20," *NTS* 12 (1965-1966): 78-80.

0404 André Feuillet, "La creation de l'univers dans le Christ d'après l'Épître aux Colossiens (1:16a)," *NTS* 12 (1965-1966): 1-9.

0405 Daniel von Allmen, "Réconciliation du monde et christologie cosmique de 2 Cor 5:14-21 à Col 1:15-23," *RHPR* 48 (1968): 32-45.

0406 F.-J. Steinmetz, "Die Weisheit und das Kreuz: Marginalien zum Kolosser- und Epheserbrief," *GeistL* 72 (1998): 112-26.

0407 Eduard Schweizer, "Christ in the Letter to the Colossians," *RevExp* 70 (1973): 451-67.

0408 Pierre Benoit, "L'hymne christologique de Col. 1,15-20. Jugement critique sur l'état des recherches," in Jacob Neusner, ed., *Christianity, Judaism and Other Greco-Roman Cults* (festschrift for Morton Smith) Part One. Leiden: Brill, 1975. Pp. 226-63.

0409 Tito Szabó, "La croce del primogenito: il primato della croce nel piano divino della creazione," in Christian Duquoc, et al., eds., *La sapienza della croce oggi, 1: la sapienza della croce nella rivelazione e nell'ecumenismo*. Turin: Elle Di Ci, 1976. Pp. 210-23.

0410 Klaus Wengst, "Versöhnung und Befreiung: ein Aspekt des Themas 'Schuld und Vergebung' im Lichte des Kolosserbriefes," *EvT* 36 (1976): 14-26.

0411 T. Evan Pollard, "Exit the Alexandrian Christ: Some Reflections on Contemporary Christology in the Light of New Testament Studies," *CANZTR* 13 (1980): 16-23.

0412 Claus Bussmann, "Gibt es christologische Begründungen für eine Unterordnung der Frau im Neuen Testament?" in Gerhard Dautzenberg, et al., eds., *Die Frau im Urchristentum*. Freiburg: Herder, 1983. Pp. 254-62.

0413 Larry R. Helyer, "Colossians 1:15-20: Pre-Pauline or Pauline?" *JETS* 26 (1983): 167-79.

0414 Christopher Rowland, "Apocalyptic Visions and the Exaltation of Christ in the Letter to the Colossians," *JSNT* 19 (1983): 73-83.

0415   Wolfgang Schenk, "Christus, das Geheimnis der Welt, als dogmatisches und ethisches Grundprinzip des Kolosserbriefes," *EvT* 43 (1983): 138-55.

0416   N. T. Wright, "Adam in Pauline Christology," *SBLSP* 22 (1983): 359-89.

0417   A. del Pérez Agua, "Derás cristológico del Salmo 110 en el Neuvo Testamento," in Marcos Fernández, et al., eds., *Simposio Biblico Español.* Madrid: Universidad Complutense, 1984. Pp. 637-62.

0418   Pierre Benoit, "Colossiens 2:2-3," in William C. Weinrich, ed., *The New Testament Age* (festschrift for Bo Reicke). 2 vols. Macon GA: Mercer Universitry Press, 1984. 1:41-51.

0419   F. F. Bruce, "Colossian Problems: The 'Christ Hymn' of Colossians 1:15-20," *BSac* 141 (1984): 99-111.

0420   Walter Kasper, "Hope in the Final Coming of Jesus Christ in Glory," *CICR* 12 (1985): 368-84.

0421   Franz Mussner, "Das Reich Christi: Bemerkungen zur Eschatologie des Corpus Paulinum," in Michael Böhnke and Hanspeter Heinz, eds., *Im Gespräch mit dem dreieinen Gott: Elemente einer trinitarischen Theologie* (festschrift for Wilhelm Breuning). Düsseldorf: Patmos Verlag, 1985. Pp. 141-55.

0422   David H. C. Read, "Gentle Jesus or Cosmic Christ," *ET* 96 (1985): 213-14.

0423   Eduard Schweizer, "Unterwegs mit meinen Lehrern," *EvT* 45 (1985): 322-37.

0424   Jan Botha, "A Stylistic Analysis of the Christ Hymn (Col 1:15-20)," in Kobus J. H. Petzer and Patrick J. Hartin, eds., *A South African Perspective on the New Testament* (festschrift for Bruce M. Metzger). Leiden: E. J. Brill, 1986. Pp. 238-51.

0425   Nikolaus Walter, "Geschichte und Mythos in der urchristlichen Präexistenzchristologie," in Hans H. Schmid, ed., *Mythos und Rationalität.* Gütersloh: Gütersloher Verlaghaus Mohn, 1988. Pp. 224-34.

0426 Michel Gourgues, "La foi chrétienne primitive face à la croix: le témoignage des formulaires pré-pauliniens," *ScE* 41 (1989): 49-69.

0427 Hugolinus Langkammer, "Jesus in der Sprache der neutestamentlichen Christuslieder," in Hubert Frankemölle and Karl Kertelge, eds., *Vom Urchristentum zu Jesus* (festschrift for Joachim Gnilka). Freiburgi: Herder, 1989. Pp. 467-86.

0428 Otto Merk, "Erwägungen zu Kol 2,6f," in Hubert Frankemölle and Karl Kertelge, eds., *Vom Urchristentum zu Jesus* (festschrift for Joachim Gnilka). Freiburgi: Herder, 1989. Pp. 407-16.

0429 Walter Wink, "The Hymn of the Cosmic Christ," in Robert T. Fortna and Beverly R. Gaventa, eds., *The Conversation Continues: Studies in Paul & John* (festschrift for Louis Martyn). Nashville: Abingdon Press, 1990. Pp. 235-45.

0430 Andrew Chester, "Jewish Messianic Expectations and Mediatorial Figures and Pauline Christology," in Martin Hengel and Ulrich Heckel, eds., *Paulus und das antike Judentum* (festschriftr for Adolf Schlatter). Tübingen: Mohr, 1991. Pp. 17-89.

0431 Isak J. Du Plessis, "Die God wat skep en herskep--ekologie en menseverhoudinge in Kolossense," *SkrifK* 12 (1991): 194-213.

0432 Andrew C. Perriman, "The Pattern of Christ's Sufferings: Colossians 1:24 and Philippians 3:10-11," *TynB* 42 (1991): 62-79.

0433 James D. G. Dunn, "The 'Body' in Colossians," in Thomas E. Schmidt and Moisés Silva, eds., *To Tell the Mystery: Essays on New Testament Eschatology* (festschrift for Robert H. Gundry). Sheffield UK: JSOT Press, 1994. Pp. 163-81.

0434 Joel B. Green and Max Turner, eds., *Jesus of Nazareth: Lord and Christ: Essays on the Historical Jesus and New Testament Christology* (festschrift Howard Marshall). Grand Rapids: Eerdmans, 1994.

0435 Roy Yates, "From Christology to Soteriology," *ET* 107 (1996): 268-70.

0436 Harold Broeckhoven, "The Social Profiles in the Colossian Debate," *JSNT* 66 (1997): 73-90.

0437 T. R. Gildmeister, "Christology and the Focus of Faith: Readings from Paul's Letter to the Colossians in Year C," *QR* 18 (1998): 89-110.

0438 E. Krentz, "κατὰ τὸν χριστόν: Preaching Colossians in Year C," *CThM* 25 (1998): 132-36.

0439 P. Jones, "L'Évangile pour l'âge du verseau: Colossiens 1:15-20," *RefRéf* 50 (1999): 13-23.

circumcision
0440 Michel van Esbroeck, "Colossians 2:11 'dans la circoncision du Christ'," in Julien Ries, et al., eds., *Gnosticisme et monde hellenistique*. Louvain-La-Neuve: Universite Catholique de Louvain, 1982. Pp. 229-35.

0441 Paul D. Gardner, "Circumcised in Baptism - Raised through Faith: A Note on Colossians 2:11-12," *WTJ* 45 (1983): 172-77.

0442 Evertt Ferguson, "Spiritual Circumcision in Early Christinaity," *SJT* 41 (1988): 485-97.

community
0443 Darrell L. Bock, " 'The New Man' as Community in Colossians and Ephesians," in Charles H. Dyer and Roy B. Zuck, eds., *Integrity of Heart, Skillfulness of Hands: biblical and Leadership Studies* (festschrift for Donald K. Campbell. Grand Rapids: Baker Book House, 1994. Pp. 157-67.

cosmology
0444 Markus Barth, "Christ and All Things," in Morna D. Hooker and Stephen G. Wilson, eds., *Paul and Paulinism* (festschrift for C. K. Barrett). London: SPCK, 1982. Pp. 160-72.

0445 Pierre Benoit, "Pauline Angelology and Demonology: Reflexions on Designations of Heavenly Powers and on Origin of Angelic Evil according to Paul," *RSB* 3 (1983): 1-18.

0446 Eduard Schweizer, "Slaves of the Elements and Worshipers of Angels," *JBL* 107 (1988): 455-68.

0447 Eduard Schweizer, "Altes und Neues zu den 'Elementen der Welt' in Kol 2,20; Gal 4,3-9," in Kurt Aland and Siegfried Meurer, eds., -

Wissenschaft und Kirche (festschrift for Eduard Lohse). Bielefeld: Luther-Verlag, 1989. Pp. 111-18.

creation

0448 Richard J. Clifford, "The Bible and the Environment," in Kevin W. Irwin and Edmund D. Pellegrino, eds., *Preserving the Creation: Environmental Theology and Ethics*. Washington: Georgetown University Press, 1994. Pp. 1-26.

crucifixion

0449 Tito Szabó, "La croce del primogenito: il primato della croce nel piano divino della creazione," in Christian Duquoc, et al., eds., *La sapienza della croce oggi, 1: la sapienza della croce nella rivelazione e nell'ecumenismo*. Turin: Elle Di Ci, 1976. Pp. 210-23.

0450 Roy Yates, "Colossians 2:15: Christ Triumphant," *NTS* 37 (1991): 573-91.

demiurge

0451 Robert M. Grant, "The Christ at the Creation," in R. Joseph Hoffmann and Gerald A Larue, eds., *Jesus in History and Myth*. Buffalo NY: Prometheus Books, 1986. Pp. 157-167.

demonology

0452 Lorenzo Bautista, "The Asian Way of Thinking in Theology," *ERT* 6 (1982): 37-49.

0453 Pierre Benoit, "Pauline Angelology and Demonology: Reflexions on Designations of Heavenly Powers and on Origin of Angelic Evil according to Paul," *RSB* 3 (1983): 1-18.

0454 Roy Yates, "Colossians 2:15: Christ Triumphant," *NTS* 37 (1991): 573-91.

deutero-Pauline

0455 Gary S. Shogren, "Presently Entering the Kingdom of Christ: The Background and Purpose of Colossians 1:12-14," *JETS* 31 (1988): 173-80.

discipleship

0456 Michael P. Knowles, " 'Christ in You, the Hope of Glory': Discipleship in Colossians," in Richard N. Longenecker, eds., *Patterns* *of Discipleship in the New Testament.* Grand Rapids: Eerdmans, 1996. Pp. 180-202.

discourse analysis

0457 Gregory T. Christopher, "A Discourse Analysis of Colossians 2:16-3:17," *GTJ* 11 (1990): 205-20.

0458 J. P. Louw, "Reading a Text as Discourse," in David A. Black, et al., eds., *Linguistics and New Testament Interpretation: Essays on Discourse Analysis.* Nashville: Broadman Press, 1992. Pp. 17-30.

ecclesiology

0459 V. Combrink and C. J. H. Venter, "Menslike subjekte in gemeente-opbou volgens die Kolossensebrief: 'n Diakoniologiese perspektief met toespitsing op eskatologiese dimensies," *In die Skriflig* 29 (1995): 583-602.

0460 Johannes L. Witte, "Die Katholizität der Kirche: eine neue Interpretation nach alter Tradition," *Greg* 42 (1961): 193-241.

0461 J. M. Efrid, *Christ, the Church, and the End: Studies in Colossians and Ephesians.* Valley Forge PA: Judson, 1980.

0462 Hartmut Löwe, "Bekenntnis, Apostelamt und Kirche im Kolosserbrief," in Dieter Lührmann and Georg Strecker, eds., *Kirche* (festschrift for Günther Bornkamm). Tübingen: Mohr, 1980. Pp. 299-314.

0463 Michel van Esbroeck, "Colossians 2:11 'dans la circoncision du Christ'," in Julien Ries, et al., eds., *Gnosticisme et monde hellenistique.* Louvain-La-Neuve: Universite Catholique de Louvain, 1982. Pp. 229-35.

0464 Leopold Sabourin, "Paul and His Thought in Recent Research," *RSB* 2 (1982): 62-73; 3 (1983): 117-31.

0465 Jean M. R. Tillard, "What Is the Church of God?" *MidS* 23 (1984): 363-80.

0466 Joseph Allen, "Renewal of the Christian Community: A Challenge for the Pastoral Ministry," *SVTQ* 29 (1985): 305-23.

0467 Gerald H. Anderson, "Christian Mission and Human Transformation: Toward Century 21," *MS* 2 (1985): 52-65.

0468 Rolf Gögler, "Inkarnationsglaube und Bibeltheologie bei Origenes," *TQ* 165 (1985): 82-94.

0469 Peter T. O'Brien, "The Church as a Heavenly and Eschatological Entity," in Don A. Carson, ed., *The Church in the Bible and the World: An International Study*. Exeter: Paternoster Press, 1987. Pp. 88-119.

0470 Joseph Sittler, "Called to Unity," *CThM* 16 (1989): 5-13.

0471 Clinton E. Arnold, "Jesus Christ: 'Head' of the Church," in Joel B. Green and Max Turner, eds., *Jesus of Nazareth: Lord and Christ: Essays on the Historical Jesus and New Testament Christology*. Grand Rapids: Eerdmans, 1994. Pp. 346-66.

0472 E. Krentz, "κατὰ τὸν χριστόν: Preaching Colossians in Year C," *CThM* 25 (1998): 132-36.

eschatology

0473 Erich Grässer, "Kol 3, 1-4 als Beispiel einer Interpretation secundum homines recipientes," *ZTK* 64 (1967): 139-68.

0474 Richard J. Bauckham, "Colossians 1:24 Again: The Apocalyptic Motif," *EQ* 47 (1975): 168-70.

0475 Ekkehard Stegemann, "Alt und neu bei Paulus und in den Deuteropaulinen (Kol-Eph)," *EvT* 37 (1977): 508-36.

0476 Roland Bergmeier, "Königlosigkeit als nachvalentinianisches Heilsprädikat," *NovT* 24 (1982): 316-39.

0477 N. T. Wright, "Adam in Pauline Christology," *SBLSP* 22 (1983): 359-89.

0478 George Johnston, "Kingdom of God Sayings in Paul's Letters," in Peter Richardson and John C. Hurd, eds., *From Jesus to Paul* (festschrift for Francis W. Beare). Waterloo: Wilfrid Laurier University Press, 1984. Pp. 143-56.

0479   Horacio E. Lona, *Die Eschatologie im Kolosser- und Epheserbrief.*
       Wurzburg: Echter Verlag, 1984.

0480   Michel Bouttier, "Petite suite paulinienne," *ETR* 60 (1985): 265-72.

0481   Walter Kasper, "Hope in the Final Coming of Jesus Christ in Glory,"
       CICR 12 (1985): 368-84.

0482   Luis F. Ladaria, "Presente y futuro en la escatología cristiana," *EE* 60
       (1985): 351-59.

0483   Franz Mussner, "Das Reich Christi: Bemerkungen zur Eschatologie
       des Corpus Paulinum," in Michael Böhnke and Hanspeter Heinz, eds.,
       *Im Gespräch mit dem dreieinen Gott: Elemente einer trinitarischen
       Theologie* (festschrift for Wilhelm Breuning). Düsseldorf: Patmos
       Verlag, 1985. Pp. 141-55.

0484   Peter T. O'Brien, "The Church as a Heavenly and Eschatological
       Entity," in Don A. Carson, ed., *The Church in the Bible and the
       World: An International Study.* Exeter: Paternoster Press, 1987. Pp.
       88-119.

0485   John R. Levison, "2 Apoc Bar 48:42-52:7 and the Apocalyptic
       Dimension of Colossians 3:1-6," *JBL* 108 (1989): 93-108.

0486   Stephen Motyer, "The Relationship between Paul's Gospel of 'All
       One in Christ Jesus' (Galatians 3:28) and the 'Household Codes',"
       VoxE 19 (1989): 33-48.

0487   Wim C. Vergeer, "Die dwaalleer in Kolosse (2): Die boodskap van die
       Kolossensebrief," *In die Skriflig* 29 (1995): 413-42.

ethics

0488   Peter Stuhlmacher, "Christliche Verantwortung bei Paulus und seinen
       Schülern," *EvT* 28 (1968): 165-86.

0489   William Lillie, "Pauline House-Tables," *ET* 86 (1975): 179-83.

0490   Fred Catherwood, "The Protestant Work Ethic: Attitude and
       Application Give it Meaning," *FundJ* 2 (1983): 22-25.

0491   Jeffery Gibbs, "The Grace of God as the Foundation for Ethics," *CTQ*
       48 (1984): 185-201.

0492   Walter H. Principe, "The Dignity and Rights of the Human Person as Saved, as Being Saved, as to Be Saved by Christ," *Greg* 65 (1984): 389-430.

0493   Daniel C. Stevens, "Christian Educational Foundations and the Pauline Triad: A Call to Faith, Hope, and Love," *CEJ* 5 (1984): 5-16.

0494   Vigen Guroian, "Seeing Worship as Ethics: An Orthodox Perspective," *JRE* 13 (1985): 332-59.

0495   Gerhard Sauter, "Leiden und 'Handeln'," *EvT* 45 (1985): 435-58.

0496   Henry J. Stob, "Natural Law Ethics: An Appraisal," *CTJ* 20 (1985): 58-68.

0497   Klaus Wengst, "Einander durch Demut für vorzüglicher zu halten: Zum Begriff 'Demut' bei Paulus und in paulinischer Tradition," in Wolfgang Schrage, ed., *Studien zum Text und zur Ethik des Neuen Testaments* (festschrift for Heinrich Greeven). Berlin: Walter de Gruyter, 1986. Pp. 428-39.

0498   Lars Hartman, "Code and Context: A Few Reflections on the Parenesis of Colossians 3:6-4:1," in Gerald F. Hawthorne and Otto Betz, eds., *Tradition and Interpretation in the New Testament* (festschrift for E. Earle Ellis). Grand Rapids MI: Eerdmans, 1987. Pp. 237-47.

0499   Anne McGuire, "Equality and Subordination in Christ: Displacing the Powers of the Household Code in Colossians," in Joseph Gower, ed., *Religion and Economic Ethics*. Lanham MD: University Press of America, 1990. Pp. 65-85.

0500   Francis Young, "The Pastoral Epistles and the Ethics of Reading," *JSNT* 45 (1992): 105-20.

0501   Wayne A. Meeks, " 'To Walk Worthily of the Lord': Moral Formation in the Pauline School Exemplified by the Letter to Colossians," in Eleonore Stump and Thomas Flint, eds., *Hermes and Athena: Biblical Exegesis and Philosophical Theology*. Notre Dame: University of Notre Dame Press, 1993. Pp. 37-58.

0502   Eleonore Stump, "Moral Authority and Pseudonymity," in Eleonore Stump and Thomas Flint, eds., *Hermes and Athena: Biblical Exegesis and Philosophical Theology*. Notre Dame: University of Notre Dame Press, 1993. Pp. 59-70.

0503   Alexander D. Hill, "Christian Character in the Marketplace: Colossians, Philemon and the Practice of Business," *Crux* 30 (1994): 27-34.

0504   Walter T. Wilson, *The Hope of Glory: Education and Exhortation in the Epistle to the Colossians*. Leiden: E. J. Brill, 1997.

faith

0505   Daniel C. Stevens, "Christian Educational Foundations and the Pauline Triad: A Call to Faith, Hope, and Love," *CEJ* 5 (1984): 5-16.

form criticism

0506   John F. Balchin, "Colossians 1:15-20: An Early Christian Hymn? The Arguments from Style," *VoxE* 15 (1985): 65-94.

0507   Lars Hartman, "Some Unorthodox Thoughts on the 'Household-Code Form'," in Jacob Neusner, et al., eds., *The Social World of Formative Christianity and Judaism* (festschrift for Howard Clark Kee). Philadelphia: Fortress Press, 1988. Pp. 219-32.

0508   Edgar Haulotte, "Formation du corpus du Nouveau Testament: recherche d'un 'module' génératif intratextuel," in Christoph Theobald, ed., *Le canon des Ecritures: études historiques, exégétiques et systématiques*. Paris: Editions du Cerf, 1990. Pp. 255-439.

gentiles

0509   Kenneth Grayston, "The Opponents in Philippians 3," *ET* 97 6 (1986): 170-72.

gnosticism

0510   Werner Förster, "Die Grundzüge der Ptolemäischen Gnosis," *NTS* 6 (1959-1960): 16-31.

0511   Dan Cockran, "A Comparative Study of the Major Teachings in Colossians and Contemporaneous Gnosticism." Master's thesis, Southwestern Baptist Theological Seminary, Fort Worth, TX, 1963.

0512   Gene L. Munn, "Introduction to Colossians," *SouJT* 16 (1973): 9-21.

0513 Roland Bergmeier, "Königlosigkeit als nachvalentinianisches Heilsprädikat," *NovT* 24 (1982): 316-39.

0514 Wayne G. Rollins, "Christological Tendenz in Colossians 1:15-20: A Theologia Crucis," in Robert F. Berkey and Sarah Edwards, eds., *Christological Perspectives* (festschrift for Harvey K. McArthur). New York: Pilgrim Press, 1982. Pp. 123-38.

0515 Ingvild S. Gilhus, "The Gnostic Demiurge: An Agnostic Trickster," *Rel* 14 (1984): 301-11.

0516 Philip J. Hefner, "God and Chaos: The Demiurge Versus the Ungrund," *Zygon* 19 (1984): 469-85.

0517 Ambrose Moyo, "The Colossian Heresy in the Light of Some Gnostic Documents from Nag Hammadi," *JTSA* 48 (1984): 30-44.

0518 W. Stephen Sabom, "The Gnostic World of Anorexia Nervosa," *JPT* 13 (1985): 243-54.

0519 Roy Yates, "Colossians and Gnosis," *JSNT* 27 (1986): 49-68.

0520 Antonio Orbe, "Deus facit, homo fit: un axioma de san Ireneo," *Greg* 69 (1988): 629-61.

0521 Jarl Fossum, "Colossians 1:15-18a in the Light of Jewish Mysticism and Gnosticism," *NTS* 35 (1989): 183-201.

0522 Michael D. Goulder, "Colossians and Barbelo," *NTS* 41 (1995): 601-19.

grace

0523 Jeffery Gibbs, "The Grace of God as the Foundation for Ethics," *CTQ* 48 (1984): 185-201.

grammar

0524 G. William Schweer, "Aoristic Revelation in the Prison Epistles," doctoral dissertation, Midwestern Baptist Theological Seminary, Kansas City KN, 1956.

0525 William C. Vaughan, "A Syntactical Analysis of the Epistles to the Colossians as an Approach to the Study of Subordinate Greek

Clauses," doctoral dissertation, Southwestern Baptist Theological
Seminary, Fort Worth TX, 1958.

haustafel
   0526   James E. Crouch, *The Origin and Intention of the Colossian
   Haustafel* Göttingen: Vandenhoeck & Ruprecht, 1972.

hellenistic influence
   0527   Karlheinz Müller, "Die Haustafel des Kolosserbriefes und das antike
   Frauenthema: Eine kritische Rückschau auf alte Ergebnisse," in
   Gerhard Dautzenberg, et al., eds., *Die Frau im Urchristentum.*
   Freiburg: Herder, 1983. Pp. 263-319.

   0528   Wayne Grudem, "Does *Kephale* ('Head') Mean 'Source' or
   'Authority over' in Greek Literature: A Survey of 2,336 Examples,"
   TriJ NS 6 (1985): 38-59.

   0529   Randal A. Argall, "The Source of a Religious Error in Colossae," *CTJ*
   22 (1987): 6-20.

   0530   Eduard Schweizer, "Slaves of the Elements and Worshipers of
   Angels," *JBL* 107 (1988): 455-68.

   0531   Eduard Schweizer, "Askese nach Kol 1,24 oder 2,20f?" in Helmut
   Merklein, ed., *Neues Testament und Ethik* (festschrift for Rudolf
   Schnackenburg). Freiburg: Herder, 1989. Pp. 340-48.

   0532   Georg Strecker, "Die neutestamentlichen Haustafeln (Kol 3,18-4,1
   und Eph 5,22-6,9)," in Helmut Merklein, ed., *Neues Testament und
   Ethik* (festschrift for Rudolf Schnackenburg). Freiburg: Herder, 1989.
   Pp. 349-75.

   0533   Daniel J. Harrington, "Christians and Jews in Colossians," in J.
   Andrew Overman, et al., eds., *Diaspora Jews and Judaism* (festschrift
   for Thomas Kraabel). Atlanta: Scholars Press, 1992. Pp. 153-61.

   0534   Dietrich Rusam, "Neue Belege zu den stoicheia tou kosmou," *ZNW*
   83 (1992): 119-25.

heresies
   0535   James S. Stewart, "First-Century Heresy and Its Modern
   Counterpart," *SJT* 23 (1970): 420-36.

0536 Craig A. Evans, "The Colossian Mystics," *Bib* 63 (1982): 188-205.

0537 Walter Schmithals, "The Corpus Paulinum and Gnosis," in A. H. B. Logan and A. J. Wedderburn, eds., *The New Testament and Gnosis* (festschrift for Robert McL. Wilson). Edinburgh: T. & T. Clark, 1983. Pp. 107-24.

0538 F. F. Bruce, "Colossian Problems: The Colossian Heresy," *BSac* 141 (1984): 195-208.

0539 Ambrose Moyo, "The Colossian Heresy in the Light of Some Gnostic Documents from Nag Hammadi," *JTSA* 48 (1984): 30-44.

0540 Roy Yates, "Colossians and Gnosis," *JSNT* 27 (1986): 49-68.

0541 Randal A. Argall, "The Source of a Religious Error in Colossae," *CTJ* 22 (1987): 6-20.

0542 H. Wayne House, "Doctrinal Issues in Colossians," *BSac* 149 (1992): 45-59, 180-92.

0543 Wim C. Vergeer, et al., "Die dwaalleer in Kolosse: 'n Konstruksie van die waarskynlike sosio-historiese en filosofiese konteks," *In die Skriflig* 28 (1994): 1-23.

holy spirit

0544 Eduard Schweizer, "Christus und Geist im Kolosserbrief2," in B. Lindars and S. S. Smalley, eds., *Christ and Spirit in the New Testament* (festschrift for C. F. D. Moule). Cambridge: University Press, 1973. Pp. 297-313.

0545 Hendrikus Berkhof, "The Holy Spirit and the World: Some Reflections on Paul's Letter to the Colossians," *JTSA* 43 (1979): 56-61.

0546 John E. Booty, "Christian Spirituality: From Wilberforce to Temple (Colossians 3:1-3)," in William J. Wolf, ed., *Angican Spirituality*. Wilton CN: Morehouse-Barlow, 1982. Pp. 69-103.

0547 Harold L. Willmington, "The Spirit of God and the Saints of God," *FundJ* 2 (1983): 43-44.

0548 Henry Ginder, "The Spirit's Empowerment in the Third Way," in Henry J. Schmidt, ed., *Witnesses of a Third Way: A Fresh Look at Evangelism*. Elgin IL: Brethren Press, 1986. Pp. 55-61.

hope
0549 G. Bornkamm, "Die Hoffnung im Kolosserbrief. Zugleich ein Beitrag zur Frage der Echtheit des Briefes," in *Geschichte und Glaube*. Münich: Kaiser, 1971. 206-13.

0550 Robert Leuenberger, "Was droben ist," *Reformatio* 21 (1972): 202-206.

0551 Ralph P. Martin, "Reconciliation and Forgiveness in Colossians," in *Reconciliation and Hope: New Testament Essays on Atonement and Eschatology* (festschrift for Leon Morris). Grand Rapids: Eerdmans, 1974. Pp. 104-24.

0552 Patrick Rogers, "Hopeful, in Spite of Chains: The Indomitable Spirit of Paul, in the Captivity Letters," *BTB* 12 (1982): 77-81.

0553 Walter Kasper, "Hope in the Final Coming of Jesus Christ in Glory," *CICR* 12 (1985): 368-84.

household duties
0554 William Lillie, "Pauline House-Tables," *ET* 86 (1975): 179-83.

0555 Karlheinz Müller, "Die Haustafel des Kolosserbriefes und das antike Frauenthema: Eine kritische Rückschau auf alte Ergebnisse," in Gerhard Dautzenberg, et al., eds., *Die Frau im Urchristentum*. Freiburg: Herder, 1983. Pp. 263-319.

0556 Lamar Cope, "On Rethinking the Philemon-Colossians Connection," *BR* 30 (1985): 45-50.

0557 Frank Stagg, "The Gospel, Haustafel, and Women: Mark 1:1; Colossians 3:18-4:1," *FM* 2 (1985): 59-63.

0558 Lars Hartman, "Code and Context: A Few Reflections on the Parenesis of Colossians 3:6-4:1," in Gerald F. Hawthorne and Otto Betz, eds., *Tradition and Interpretation in the New Testament* (festschrift for E. Earle Ellis). Grand Rapids MI: Eerdmans, 1987. Pp. 237-47.

0559 Lars Hartman, "Some Unorthodox Thoughts on the 'Household-Code Form'," in Jacob Neusner, et al., eds., *The Social World of Formative Christianity and Judaism* (festschrift for Howard Clark Kee). Philadelphia: Fortress Press, 1988. Pp. 219-32.

0560 Orsay Groupe, "Une lecture féministe des 'codes domestiques'," *FV* 88 (1989): 59-69.

0561 Stephen Motyer, "The Relationship between Paul's Gospel of 'All One in Christ Jesus' (Galatians 3:28) and the 'Household Codes'," - *VoxE* 19 (1989): 33-48.

0562 R. Scott Nash, "Heuristic Haustafeln: Domestic Codes as Entrance to the Social World of Early Christianity: The Case of Colossians," in Jacob Neusner, et al., eds., *Religious Writings and Religious Systems: Systemic Analysis of Holy Books*. Volume 2. *Christianity*. Atlanta: Scholars Press, 1989. Pp. 25-50.

0563 Georg Strecker, "Die neutestamentlichen Haustafeln (Kol 3,18-4,1 und Eph 5,22-6,9)," in Helmut Merklein, ed., *Neues Testament und Ethik* (festschrift for Rudolf Schnackenburg). Freiburg: Herder, 1989. Pp. 349-75.

0564 Anne McGuire, "Equality and Subordination in Christ: Displacing the Powers of the Household Code in Colossians," in Joseph Gower, ed., *Religion and Economic Ethics*. Lanham MD: University Press of America, 1990. Pp. 65-85.

0565 Roy Yates, "The Christian Way of Life: The Paraenetic Material in Colossians 3:1-4:6," *EQ* 63 (1991): 241-51.

humility
0566 Fred O. Francis, "Humility and Angelic Worship in Colossians 2:18," *StTheol* 16 (1962): 109-34.

hymns
0567 S. de Ausejo, "Es un himno a Cristo el prólogo de San Juan? Los himnos cristologicos de la Iglesia primitiva y el prólogo del IV Evangelio Qn., 1, 18," in *La escatología individual neotestamentaria a la luz de las ideas en los tiempos apostolicos*. Madrid: Liberia, 1956. Pp. 307-96.

0568 J. M. Robinson, "A Formal Analysis of Colossians 1:15-20," *JBL* 76 (1957): 270-87.

0569 Werner Förster, "Die Grundzüge der Ptolemäischen Gnosis," *NTS* 6 (1959-1960): 16-31.

0570 J. Jervell, "Zu Kol 1,15-20. Gott in Christus II," in *Imago Dei: Gen 1.26f im Spätjudentum, in der Gnosis und in den paulinischen Briefen.* FRLANT #76. Göttingen: Vandenhoeck & Ruprecht, 1960. Pp. 218-26.

0571 Ernst Bammel, "Versuch zu Col 1,15-20," *ZNW* 52 (1961): 88-95.

0572 Harald Hegermann, *Die Vorstellung vom Schopfungsmittler im hellinistischen Judentum und Urchristentum.* Berlin, Akademie-Verlag, 1961.

0573 D. M. Stanley, "A Hymn from the Early Christian Liturgy. Colossians 1:13-20," in *Christ's Resurrection in Pauline Soteriology.* Rome: Pontifical Institute Press, 1961. Pp. 202-208.

0574 Paul Ellingworth, "Colossians i. 15-20 and Its Context," *ET* 73 (1961-1962): 252-53.

0575 James H. Burtness, "All the Fulness," *Dia* 3 (1964): 257-63.

0576 G. W. H. Lampe, "New Testament Doctrine of *Ktisis*," *SJT* 17 (1964): 449-62.

0577 Ralph P. Martin, "An Early Christian Hymn," *EQ* 36 (1964): 195-205.

0578 G. Schille, "Kolosser 2, 9-15,"in *Frühchristliche Hymnen.* Berlin: Evangelische Verlagsanstalt, 1965. Pp. 31-37.

0579 Fred B. Craddock, "All Things in Him--A Critical Note on Colossians 1:15-20," *NTS* 12 (1965-1966): 78-80.

0580 R. Deichgräber, "Kolosser 1, 15-20," in *Gotteshymnus und Christushymmis in der frühen Christenheit: Untersuchungen zu Form, Sprache und Stil der frühchristlichen Hymnus.* Göttingen: Vandenhoeck & Ruprecht, 1967. Pp. 143-55.

0581 Daniel von Allmen, "Réconciliation du monde et christologie cosmique de 2 Cor 5:14-21 à Col 1:15-23," *RHPR* 48 (1968): 32-45.

0582 Eduard Lohse, "Ein hymnisches Bekenntnis in Kol 2,13-15," in A.-L. Descamps and André Halleux, eds., *Mélanges bibliques en hommage au R. P. Béda Rigaux*. Gembloux: Duculot, 1970. Pp. 427-35.

0583 J. T. Sanders, *The New Testament Christological Hymns: Their Historical-Religious Background*. Cambridge: University Press, 1971. Pp. 12-14, 75-87.

0584 B. Vawter, "The Colossians Hymn and the Principle of Redaction," *CBQ* 33 (1971): 62-81.

0585 Wolfgang Pöhlmann, "Die hymnischen All-Prädikationen in Kol 1:15-20," *ZNW* 64 (1973): 53-74.

0586 Peter T. O'Brien, "Colossians 1:20 and the Reconciliation of All Things," *RTR* 33 (1974): 45-53.

0587 Pierre Benoit, "L'hymne christologique de Col. 1,15-20. Jugement critique sur l'état des recherches," in Jacob Neusner, ed., *Christianity, Judaism and Other Greco-Roman Cults* (festschrift for Morton Smith) Part One. Leiden: Brill, 1975. Pp. 226-63.

0588 C. Burger, "Der Hymnus in Kolosser 1,15-20," in *Schöpfung und Versöhnung*. Neukrichen-Vluyn: Neukrichener Verlag, 1975. Pp. 3-114.

0589 C. Burger, *Schöpfung und Versöhnung: Studien zum liturgischen Gui im Kolosser- und Epheserbrief*. WMANT #46. Neukirchen-Vluyn: Neukirchener, 1975.

0590 E. H. Maly, "Creation in the New Testament," in Miriam Ward, ed., *Biblical Studies in Contemporary Thought*. Burlington VT: Trinity College Biblical Institute, 1975. Pp. 104-12.

0591 J.-N. Aletti, "Créés dans le Christ," *Chr* 23 (1976): 343-56.

0592 P. Dacquino, "Cristo Figlio di Dio e Figlio dell'Uomo," in *Studia Hiorosolyrnitana. I. Studi archeologici* (festschrift for Bellarmino Bagatti). Jerusalem: Francisan Press, 1976. Pp. 135-45.

0593   A. di Giovanni, "Impianto teoretico e struttura dialettica di Col. 1, 15-20," in *La Cristologia in san Paolo*. Brescia: Paideia, 1976. Pp. 247-56.

0594   P. Grech, "L'inno cristologico di Col. 1 e la gnosi," in *La Cristologia in san Paolo*. Brescia: Paideia, 1976. Pp. 81-95.

0595   Stanislas Lyonnet, "Ruolo cosmico di Cristo in Col. 1, 15ss. in luce di quello della Tora nel giudaismo," in *La Cristologia in san Paolo*. Brescia: Paideia, 1976. Pp. 57-79.

0596   F. Montagnini, "Linee di convergenza fra la sapienza vetertestamentaria e l'inno cristologico di Col. 1," in *La Cristologia in san Paolo*. Brescia: Paideia, 1976. Pp. 37-56

0597   P. Rossano, "Riflessi ecumenici di Cristo secondo Col. 1, 15-20," in *La Cristologia in san Paolo*. Brescia: Paideia, 1976. Pp. 382-84.

0598   G. Segalla, "L'inno cristologico di Col. 1,15-20 nel quadro degli altri inni e della cristologia paolina," in *La Cristologia in san Paolo*. Brescia: Paideia, 1976. Pp. 375-77.

0599   Tito Szabó, "La croce del primogenito: il primato della croce nel piano divino della creazione," in Christian Duquoc, et al., eds., *La sapienza della croce oggi, 1: la sapienza della croce nella rivelazione e nell'ecumenismo*. Turin: Elle Di Ci, 1976. Pp. 210-23.

0600   F. Manns, "Col. 1,15-20 inidrash chrétien de Gen. 1,1," *RevSR* 53 (1979): 100-10.

0601   Wayne McCown, "The Hymnic Structure of Colossians 1:15-20," *EQ* 51 (1979): 156-62.

0602   Larry R. Helyer, "Colossians 1:15-20: Pre-Pauline or Pauline?" *JETS* 26 (1983): 167-79.

0603   Wolfgang Schenk, "Christus, das Geheimnis der Welt, als dogmatisches und ethisches Grundprinzip des Kolosserbriefes," *EvT* 43 (1983): 138-55.

0604   F. F. Bruce, "Colossian Problems: The 'Christ Hymn' of Colossians 1:15-20," *BSac* 141 (1984): 99-111.

0605 Ingvild S. Gilhus, "The Gnostic Demiurge: An Agnostic Trickster," *Rel* 14 (1984): 301-11.

0606 John F. Balchin, "Colossians 1:15-20: An Early Christian Hymn? The Arguments from Style," *VoxE* 15 (1985): 65-94.

0607 Steven M. Baugh, "The Poetic Form of Colossians 1:15-20," *WTJ* 47 No 2 (1985): 227-44.

0608 Jan Botha, "A Stylistic Analysis of the Christ Hymn (Col 1:15-20)," in Kobus J. H. Petzer and Patrick J. Hartin, eds., *A South African Perspective on the New Testament* (festschrift for Bruce M. Metzger). Leiden: E. J. Brill, 1986. Pp. 238-51.

0609 Hugolinus Langkammer, "Jesus in der Sprache der neutestamentlichen Christuslieder," in Hubert Frankemölle and Karl Kertelge, eds., *Vom Urchristentum zu Jesus* (festschrift for Joachim Gnilka). Freiburgi: Herder, 1989. Pp. 467-86.

0610 Edgar Haulotte, "Formation du corpus du Nouveau Testament: recherche d'un 'module' génératif intratextuel," in Christoph Theobald, ed., *Le canon des Ecritures: études historiques, exégétiques et systématiques.* Paris: Editions du Cerf, 1990. Pp. 255-439.

0611 Robert J. Karris, *A Symphony of New Testament Hymns: Commentary on Philippians 2:5-11, Colossians 1:15-20, Ephesians 2:14-16, 1 Timothy 3:16, Titus 3:4-7, 1 Peter 3:18-22, and 2 Timothy 2:11-13.* Collegeville MN: Liturgical Press, 1996.

0612 C. Basevi, "Col 1:15-20: Las posibles fuentes del 'himmo' cristológico y su importamcia para la interpretación," *ScripT* 30 (1998): 779-802.

0613 E. Krentz, "κατά τὸν χριστόν: Preaching Colossians in Year C," *CThM* 25 (1998): 132-36.

inspiration

0614 Rolf Gögler, "Inkarnationsglaube und Bibeltheologie bei Origenes," *TQ* 165 (1985): 82-94.

introduction
0615   Heinrich Lisco, *Vincula sanctorum: ein Beitrag zur Erklarung der Gefangenschaftsbriefe des Apostels Paulus*. Berlin: F. Schneider, 1900.

0616   Orello Cone, *The Epistles to the Hebrews, Colossians, Ephesians, and Philemon, the Pastoral Epistles, the Epistles of James, Peter, and Jude together with a Sketch of the History of the Canon of the New Testament*. New York: G. P. Putnam, 1901.

0617   Alphons A. Steinmann, *Gegen welche Irrlehrer richtet sich der Kolosserbrief?* Strassburg: Druck von F. X. Le Roux & Co., 1906.

0618   John Rutherford, *St. Paul's Epistles to Colossae and Laodicea: The Epistle to the Colossians Viewed in Relation to the Epistle to the Ephesians*. Eninburgh: T. & T. Clark, 1908.

0619   L. H. Hough, "The Message of the Epistles - Colossians," *ET* 45 (1933-1934): 103-108.

0620   Werner Ochel, *Die Annahme einer Bearbeitung des Kolosser-Briefes im Epheser-Brief in einer Analyse des Epheser-Briefes untersucht*. Würzburg: K. Triltsch, 1934.

0621   George S. Duncan, "The Epistles of the Imprisonment in Recent Discussion," *ET* 46 (1934-1935): 293-98.

0622   F. von Bodelschwingh, *Das Geheimnis und die Fulle Christi in der Heilsgeschichte: nach dem Kolosser-Brief*. Bethel bei Bielefeld: Verlagshandlung der Anstalt Bethel, 1936.

0623   Max A. Wagenfuhrer, *Die Bedeutung Christi für Welt und Kirche: Studien zum Koloser- und Epheserbrief*. Leipzig: Otto Wigand'sche Buchdruckerei, 1941.

0624   E. Percy, *Die Probleme der Kolosser- und Epheserbriefe*. Lund: Gleerup, 1946.

0625   E. Lewis, "Paul and the Perverters of Christianity. Revelation Through the Epistle to the Colossians ," *Int* 2 (1948): 143.

0626   E. Percy, "Zu den Problemen des Kolosser- und Epheserbriefes," *ZNW* 43 (1950-1951): 178-94.

0627   Werner Bieder, *Die kolossische Irrlehre und die Kirche von heute.* Zollikon: Evangelischer Verlag, 1952.

0628   Heinz Hunger, *Paulus im Gefangnis: die Gedankengange der Briefe des Apostels an Philemon und die Gemeinden in Kolossa, Ephesus und Philippi.* Bielefeld: Ludwig Bechauf Verlag: 1953.

0629   J. E. Uitman, *Christus het Hoofd: de brief aan de Colossenzen.* Nijkerk: G. F. Callenbach, 1955.

0630   George S. Duncan, "An Important Hypotheses Reconsidered- VI, Were Paul's Imprisonment Epistles Written from Ephesus?" *ET* 67 (1955-1956): 163-66.

0631   J. M. Gonzalez Ruiz, "Las asambleas cultuales en las epístolas de la cautividad," in *La escatología individual neotestamentaria a la luz de las ideas en los tiempos apostolicos.* Madrid: Libería, 1956. Pp. 291-306.

0632   Eduard Schweizer, "Zur Frage der Echtheit des Kolosser- und des Epheserbriefes," *ZNW* 47 (1956): 287.

0633   J. Coutts, "The Relationship of Ephesians and Colossians," *NTS* 4 (1957-1958): 201-207.

0634   G. Bornkamm, "Die Häresie des Kolosserbriefes," in *Das Ende des Gesetzes.* Münich: Kaiser, 1959. Pp. 139-56.

0635   G. Bornkamm, "Die Hoffnung im Kolosserbrief - Zugleich ein Beitrag zur Frage der Echtheit des Briefes," in *Studien zum Neuen Testament und zur Patristik* (festschrift for Erich Klostermann). Berlin: Akademie-Verlag, 1961. Pp. 1-8.

0636   Emanuel Frautschi, *Jesus Christus Allein; eine auslegung des Kilosserbriefes* Bern: Christliches Verlagshaus, 1961.

0637   J. Gewiess, "Die apologetische Methode des Apostels Paulus gegen die Irrlehre in Kolossä," *BibL* 3 (1962): 258-70.

0638   H. Paradis, "Le Christ Tête de l'Église, selon les epîtres aux Colossiens et aux Éphésiens," in *L'Église dans la Bible.* Burges: Desclée de Brouwer, 1962. Pp. 95-115.

0639 Klaus Wengst, "Der Kolosser- und der Epheserbrief und ihr Traditionsdenken," in *Das Verständnis der Tradition bei Paulus und in den Deuteropaulinen*. Neukrichen-Vluyn: Neukrichener Verlag, 1962. Pp. 121-32.

0640 W. Barclay, *The All-sufficient Christ. Studies in Paul's Letter to the Colossians*. London: SCM Press, 1963.

0641 Eduard Lohse, "Christologie und Ethik im Kolosserbrief," in *Apophoreta* (festschrift for Ernst Haenchen). Berlin: Töpelmann, 1964. Pp. 157-68.

0642 Eduard Lohse, "Christusherrschaft und Kirche im Kolosserbrief," *NTS* 11 (1964-1965): 203-16.

0643 Heinrich Langenberg, *Der Kolosserbrief: die Grosse des Christus und die hohe Berufung der Gemeinde*. Hamburg: Schriftenmission Achtel, 1965.

0644 Froedrich Minckwitz, *Die Gnade sei mit euch: Gedanken zum Brief des Apostels Paulus an die Gemeinde in Kolossa*. Leipzig: St. Benno, 1965.

0645 F. F. Bruce, "St. Paul in Rome. 3. The Epistle to the Colossians," *BJRL* 48 (1965-1966): 268-85.

0646 Udo Borse, *Der Kolosserbrieftext des Pelagius*. Bonn: Druck: Rheinische Friedrich-Wilhelms-Universitat, 1966.

0647 Werner Förster, "Die Irrlehrer des Kolosserbriefes," in *Studia Biblica et Semitica*. Wageningen: Veenman, 1966. Pp. 71-80.

0648 E. P. Sanders, "Literary Dependence in Colossians," *JBL* 85 (1966): 28-45.

0649 P. Dacquino, "Laiettera ai Colossesi," in *Il messaggio della salvezza: Corso completo di studi biblici*. 5 volumes. Elle di ci: Torino-Leumann, 1966-1970. 5:675-97.

0650 R. S. Barbour, "Salvation and Cosmology: The Setting of the Epistle to the Colossians," *SJT* 20 (1967): 257-71.

0651 R. C. Tannehill, "Ephesians and Colossians," in *Dying and Rising with Christ: A Study in Pauline Theology.* Berlin: Töpelmann, 1967. Pp. 47-54.

0652 Eduard Lohse, "Pauline Theology in the Letter to the Colossians," *NTS* 15 (1968-1969): 211-20.

0653 Gunnar Bonsaksen, *Streiflys over Kolossenserbrevet.* Kristiansand: Evangelistens Forlag, 1969.

0654 F.-J. Steinmetz, *Protologische Heils-Zuversicht. Die Strukturen des soteriologischen und christologischen Denkens im Kolosserund Epheserbrief.* Frankfurt: Josef Knecht, 1969.

0655 G. Bornkamm, "Die Hoffnung im Kolosserbrief. Zugleich ein Beitrag zur Frage der Echtheit des Briefes," in *Geschichte und Glaube.* Münich: Kaiser, 1971. 206-13.

0656 J. Lähnemann, *Der Kolosserbrief: Komposition, Situation und Argumentation.* Studien zum Neuen Testament #3. Gütersloh, Mohn, 1971.

0657 J. Bradley, "The Religious Life-Setting of the Epistle to the Colossians," *SBT* 2 (1972): 17-36.

0658 C. Noyen, "Foi, charité, espérance et 'connaissance' dans les Épîtres de la Captivite," 11 *NRT* 94 (1972): 897-911, 1031-52.

0659 H. Weiss, "The Law in the Epistle to the Colossians," *CBQ* 34 (1972): 294-314.

0660 William L. Hendricks, "All in All: Theological Themes in Colossians," *SouJT* 16 (1973): 23-35.

0661 Gene L. Munn, "Introduction to Colossians," *SouJT* 16 (1973): 9-21.

0662 John B. Polhill, "Relationship between Ephesians and Colossians," - *RevExp* 70 (1973): 439-50.

0663 Bo Reicke, "Historical Setting of Colossians," *RevExp* 70 (1973): 429-38.

0664 Eduard Schweizer, "Christus und Geist im Kolosserbrief," in B. Lindars and S. S. Smalley, eds., *Christ and Spirit in the New Testament* (festschrift for C. F. D. Moule). Cambridge: University Press, 1973. Pp. 297-313.

0665 C. W. Scudder, "Colossians Speaks to Contemporary Culture," *SouJT* 16 (1973): 37-48.

0666 A. J. Bandstra, "Did the Colossian Errorist Need a Mediator?" in R. N. Longenecker and M. C. Tenney, eds., *New Dimensions in New Testament Study*. Grand Rapids: Zondervan, 1974. Pp. 329-43.

0667 Ralph P. Martin, "Reconciliation and Forgiveness in Colossians," in *Reconciliation and Hope: New Testament Essays on Atonement and Eschatology* (festschrift for Leon Morris). Grand Rapids: Eerdmans, 1974. Pp. 104-24.

0668 P. Cambouropoulos, "The Colossian Heresy and its Life-Situation in the Epistle to the Colossians," *SBT* 5 (1975): 69-70.

0669 Fred O. Francis, *Conflict at Colossae: A Problem in the Interpretation of Early Christianity*. Rev. ed. Missoula MT: Scholars Press, 1975.

0670 P. Lamarche, "Structure de l'Épître aux Colossiens," *Bib* 56 (1975): 453-63.

0671 S. Dockx, "Authenticité des lettres de la captivité," in *Chronologies néotestamentaires et Vie de l'Église primitive*. Gembloux: Duculot, 1976. Pp. 179-87.

0672 Eduard S chweizer, "Christianity of the Circumcised and Judaism of the Uncircumcised: The Background of Matthew and Colossians," in Robert Hamerton- Kelly and R. Scroggs, eds., *Jews, Greeks and Christians: Religious Cultures in Late Antiquity* (festschrift for William David Davies). Leiden: Brill, 1976. Pp. 245-60.

0673 Eduard Schweizer, "The Letter to the Colossians neither Pauline nor Post-Pauline?" in *Pluralisme et oecuménisme en recherches théologiques* (festschrift for R. P. Dockx). BETL #43. Gembloux: Duculot, 1976. Pp. 3-16.

0674 William L. Lane, "Creed and Theology: Reflections on Colossians," *JETS* 21 (1978): 213-20.

0675 G. Schille, *Das alteste Paulus-Bild: Beobachtungen zur lukanischen und zur deuteropaulinischen Paulus-Darstellung.* Berlin: Evangelische Verlagsanstalt, 1979.

0676 J. M. Efrid, *Christ, the Church, and the End: Studies in Colossians and Ephesians.* Valley Forge PA: Judson, 1980.

0677 Wilbur N. Pickering, *A Framework for Discourse Analysis.* Dallas TX: Summer Institute of Linguistics, 1980.

0678 Roy Yates, "Christ and the Powers of Evil in Colossians," *StudB* 3 (1980): 461-68.

0679 Joachim Gnilka, "Das Paulusbild im Kolosser: und Epheserbrief," in Paul Mueller and Werner Stenger, eds., *Kontinuitaet und Einheit* (festschrift for Franz Mussner). Freiburg: Herder, 1981. Pp. 179-93.

0680 H. Merklein, "Paulinische Theologie in der Rezeption des Kolosser- und 1 Epheserbriefes," in Karl Kertelge, ed., *Paulus in den neutestamentlichen Spätschriften.* Freiburg: Herder, 1981. Pp. 25-69.

0681 G. de Ru, *Heeft het lijden van Christus aanvulling nodig?: onderzoek naar de interpretatie van Colossenzen 1:24.* Amsterdam: Ton Bolland, 1981.

0682 G. E. Cannon, *The Use of Traditional Materials in Colossians.* Macon GA: Mercer University Press, 1983.

0683 F. F. Bruce, "Colossian Problems: Jews and Christians in the Lycus Valley," *BSac* 141 (1984): 3-15.

0684 T. Y. Mullins, "The Thanksgivings of Philemon and Colossians," *NTS* 30 (1984): 288-93.

0685 Charles M. Nielsen, "The Status of Paul and His Letters in Colossians," *PRS* 12 (1985): 103-22.

0686 Mark C. Kiley, *Colossians as Pseudepigraphy.* Sheffield: JSOT Press, 1986.

0687   Harlyn J. Kuschel, *Philippians, Colossians, Philemon.* Milwaukee:
            Northwestern Publishing House, 1986.

0688   Mario Masini, *Filippesi, Colossesi, Efesini, Filemone: le lettere della
            prigionia.* Brescia: Queriniana, 1987.

0689   Peter Muller, *Anfange der Paulusschule: dargestellt am zweiten
            Thessalonicherbrief und am Kolosserbrief.* Zurich: Theologischer
            Verlag, 1988.

0690   Phillip Melanchthon, *Paul's Letter to the Colossians.* Sheffield:
            Almond Press, 1989.

0691   J. H. Roberts, "Navorsingsberig: 'n kommentaar, Filemon en
            Kolossense," *ThEv* 22 (1989): 14-20.

0692   Gjertrud Schnackenberg, "The Epistle of Paul the Apostle to the
            Colossians," in Alfred Corn, ed., *Incarnation: Contemporary Writers
            on the New Testament.* New York: Viking, 1990. Pp. 189-211.

0693   Walter Wink, "The Hymn of the Cosmic Christ," in Robert T. Fortna
            and Beverly R. Gaventa, eds., *The Conversation Continues: Studies
            in Paul & John* (festschrift for Louis Martyn). Nashville: Abingdon
            Press, 1990. Pp. 235-45.

0694   George W. Knight, "Husbands and Wives as Analogues of Christ and
            the Church: Ephesians 5:21-33 and Colossians 3:18-19," in John Piper
            and Wayne A. Grudem, eds., *Recovering Biblical Manhood and
            Womanhood: A Response to Evangelical Feminism.* Wheaton:
            Crossway Books, 1991. Pp. 165-78; 492-95.

0695   J. P. Louw, "Reading a Text as Discourse," in David A. Black, et al.,
            eds., *Linguistics and New Testament Interpretation: Essays on
            Discourse Analysis.* Nashville: Broadman Press, 1992. Pp. 17-30.

0696   Edward C. Wharton, *Christ and the Church: The Fulfillment of
            Purpose and Prophecy.* West Monroe LA: Howard Publishing, 1992.

0697   Peter Dschulnigg, "Schöpfung im Licht des Neuen Testaments:
            Neutestamentliche Schöpfungsaussagen und ihre Funktion," *FZPT* 40
            (1993): 125-45.

0698 Arland J. Hultgren, "Colossians," in Gerhard A. Krodel, eds., *The Deutero-Pauline Letters: Ephesians, Colossians, 2 Thessalonians, 1-2 Timothy, Titus*. Minneapolis: Fortress Press, 1993. Pp. 24-38.

0699 Gerhard A. Krodel, ed., *The Deutero-Pauline Letters: Ephesians, Colossians, 2 Thessalonians, 1-2 Timothy, Titus*. Minneapolis: Fortress Press, 1993.

0700 Clément Legaré, "La dimension pathémique dans l'Épître aux Colossiens," in Louis Panier, ed., *Le temps de la lecture: exégèse biblique et sémiotique* (festschrift for Jean Delorme). Paris, Cerf, 1993. Pp. 215-27.

0701 Eleonore Stump and Thomas Flint, eds., *Hermes and Athena: Biblical Exegesis and Philosophical Theology*. Notre Dame: University of Notre Dame Press, 1993.

0702 Richard E. DeMaris, *The Colossian Controversy: Wisdom in Dispute at Colossae*. Sheffield: JSOT Press, 1994.

0703 Clinton E. Arnold, *The Colossian Syncretism: The Interface between Christianity and Folk Belief at Colossae*. Tübingen: J.C.B. Mohr, 1995.

0704 Andreas Dettwiler, "L'Épître aux Colossiens: un exemple de réception de la théologie Paulinienne," *FV* 94 (1995): 27-40.

0705 Lars Hartman, "Humble and Confident: On the So-Called Philosophers in Colossae," in David Hellholm, et al., eds., *Mighty Minorities?: Mminorities in Early Christianity - Positions and Strategies* (festschrift for Jacob Jervell). Oslo: Scandinavian University Press, 1995. Pp. 25-39.

0706 Jennifer Maclean, "Ephesians and the Problem of Colossians: Interpretation of Texts and Traditions in Ephesians 1:1-2:10," doctoral dissertation, Harrvard University, Cambridge MA, 1995.

0707 James D. G. Dunn, "Deutero-Pauline Letters," in John M. G. Barclay and John P. M. Sweet, eds., *Early Christian Thought in Its Jewish Context* (festschrift for Morna D. Hooker). New York: Cambridge University Press, 1996. Pp. 130-44.

0708   Troy Martin, *By Philosophy and Empty Deceit: Colossians as Response to a Cynic Critique*. Sheffield: Sheffield Academic Press, 1996.

0709   Angela Standhartinger, *Studien zur Entstehungsgeschichte und Intention des Kolosserbriefs*. Leiden; Boston: Brill, 1999.

Judaziers
0710   Kenneth Grayston, "The Opponents in Philippians 3," *ET* 97 6 (1986): 170-72.

justification
0711   Traian Valdman, "Uno sguardo ortodosso sulla giustificazione in Lutero," *SEcu* 1 (1983): 277-88.

0712   Timothy J. Wengert, *Human Freedom, Christian Righteousness: Philip Melanchthon's Exegetical Dispute with Erasmus of Rotterdam*. New York: Oxford University Press, 1998.

kerygma
0713   Henry Ginder, "The Spirit's Empowerment in the Third Way," in Henry J. Schmidt, ed., *Witnesses of a Third Way: A Fresh Look at Evangelism*. Elgin IL: Brethren Press, 1986. Pp. 55-61.

Kingdom of God
0714   George Johnston, "Kingdom of God Sayings in Paul's Letters," in Peter Richardson and John C. Hurd, eds., *From Jesus to Paul* (festschrift for Francis W. Beare). Waterloo: Wilfrid Laurier University Press, 1984. Pp. 143-56.

0715   Franz Mussner, "Das Reich Christi: Bemerkungen zur Eschatologie des Corpus Paulinum," in Michael Böhnke and Hanspeter Heinz, eds., *Im Gespräch mit dem dreieinen Gott: Elemente einer trinitarischen Theologie* (festschrift for Wilhelm Breuning). Düsseldorf: Patmos Verlag, 1985. Pp. 141-55.

law
0716   H. Weiss, "The Law in the Epistle to the Colossians," *CBQ* 34 (1972): 294-314.

0717   F. F. Bruce, "Colossian Problems: Christ as Conqueror and Reconciler," *BSac* 141 (1984): 291-302.

Lord's Supper

0718 John E. Booty, "Christian Spirituality: From Wilberforce to Temple (Colossians 3:1-3)," in William J. Wolf, ed., *Angican Spirituality*. Wilton CN: Morehouse-Barlow, 1982. Pp. 69-103.

0719 Vigen Guroian, "Seeing Worship as Ethics: An Orthodox Perspective," *JRE* 13 (1985): 332-59.

0720 John D. Laurence, "The Eucharist as the Imitation of Christ," *TS* 47 (1986): 286-96.

love

0721 Daniel C. Stevens, "Christian Educational Foundations and the Pauline Triad: A Call to Faith, Hope, and Love," *CEJ* 5 (1984): 5-16.

Luke, the individual

0722 W. D. Thomas, "Luke, the Beloved Physician (Col 4,5)," *ET* 95 (1983-1984): 279-81.

marriage

0723 Bernhard Hanssler, "Autorität in der Kirche," *IKaZ* 14 (1985): 493-504.

0724 Jean Y. Thériault, "La femme chrétienne dans les textes pauliniens," *ScE* 37 (1985): 297-317.

0725 John Piper and Wayne A. Grudem, eds., *Recovering Biblical Manhood and Womanhood: A Response to Evangelical Feminisma*. Wheaton: Crossway Books, 1991.

missions

0726 Eugene W. Bunkowske, "Was Luther a Missionary?" *CTQ* 49 (1985): 161-79.

Nag Hammadi

0727 Gedaliahu A. G. Stroumsa, "Form(s) of God: Some Notes on *Metatron* and Christ," *HTR* 76 (1983): 269-88.

paraenesis

0728 Roy Yates, "The Christian Way of Life: The Paraenetic Material in Colossians 3:1-4:6," *EQ* 63 (1991): 241-51.

0729   Wayne A. Meeks, " 'To Walk Worthily of the Lord': Moral Formation in the Pauline School Exemplified by the Letter to Colossians," in Eleonore Stump and Thomas Flint, eds., *Hermes and Athena: Biblical Exegesis and Philosophical Theology*. Notre Dame: University of Notre Dame Press, 1993. Pp. 37-58.

passion

0730   William L. Craig, "The Historicity of the Empty Tomb of Jesus," *NTS* 31 (1985): 39-67.

0731   Gerhard Sauter, "Leiden und 'Handeln'," *EvT* 45 (1985): 435-58.

peace

0732   Leopold Sabourin, "Paul and His Thought in Recent Research," *RSB* 2 (1982): 62-73; 3 (1983): 117-31.

0733   Richard D. Patterson, "Peace, Part 2," *FundJ* 3 (1984): 59.

perseverance

0734   Robert A. Peterson, "The Perseverance of the Saints: A Theological Exegesis of Four Key New Testament Passages," *Pres* 17 (1991): 95-112.

person and work of Christ

0735   Ralph M. Smith, "An Inquiry into the Nature of the Person and Work of Christ as Revealed in the Imprisonment Epistles," doctoral dissertation, Southwestern Baptist Theological Seminary, Fort Worth TX, 1960.

prayer

0736   Paul Kalluveettil, "Prayer as Celebration: Towards the Merging of the Divine Human Milieus in the Bible," *JDharma* 10 (1985): 258-79.

0737   John H. P. Reumann, "How Do We Interpret 1 Timothy 2:1-5?" in H. George Anderson, et al., eds., *The One Mediator, the Saints, and Mary*. Minneapolis: Augsburg, 1992. Pp. 149-57.

Qumran scrolls

0738   Steven M. Baugh, "The Poetic Form of Colossians 1:15-20," *WTJ* 47 No 2 (1985): 227-44.

0739 Gary S. Shogren, "Presently Entering the Kingdom of Christ: The Background and Purpose of Colossians 1:12-14," *JETS* 31 (1988): 173-80.

reconciliation

0740 Daniel von Allmen, "Réconciliation du monde et christologie cosmique de 2 Cor 5:14-21 à Col 1:15-23," *RHPR* 48 (1968): 32-45.

0741 Ralph P. Martin, "Reconciliation and Forgiveness in Colossians," in *Reconciliation and Hope: New Testament Essays on Atonement and Eschatology* (festschrift for Leon Morris). Grand Rapids: Eerdmans, 1974. Pp. 104-24.

0742 Peter T. O'Brien, "Colossians 1:20 and the Reconciliation of All Things," *RTR* 33 (1974): 45-53.

0743 Markus Barth, "Christ and All Things," in Morna D. Hooker and Stephen G. Wilson, eds., *Paul and Paulinism* (festschrift for C. K. Barrett). London: SPCK, 1982. Pp. 160-72.

0744 Cesare C. Marcheselli, "La struttura letteraria di Col 1:(14b); 1:15-20a, b, 1, 2 la celebrazione cultuale della funzionalità ministeriale del primato-servizio di Gesù Cristo Signore," in C. C. Marcheselli, ed., *Parola e spirito* (festschrift for Settimio Cipriani). Volume 1. Brescia: Paideia Editrice, 1982. Pp. 497-519.

0745 Larry R. Helyer, "Colossians 1:15-20: Pre-Pauline or Pauline?" *JETS* 26 (1983): 167-79.

0746 F. F. Bruce, "Colossian Problems: Christ as Conqueror and Reconciler," *BSac* 141 (1984): 291-302.

0747 Gerald H. Anderson, "Christian Mission and Human Transformation: Toward Century 21," *MS* 2 (1985): 52-65.

0748 Anne Etienne, "Réconciliation: un aspect de la théologie paulinienne," *FV* 84 (1985):49-57.

redemption

0749 G. W. H. Lampe, "New Testament Doctrine of *Ktisis*," *SJT* 17 (1964): 449-62.

0750 Kurt Scharf, "Scope of the Redemptive Task, Colossians 1:15-20," *CTM* 36 (1965): 291-300.

0751 Thomas J. Sappington, *Revelation and Redemption at Colossae.* Sheffield: JSOT Press, 1991.

regeneration
0752 C. F. D. Moule, "New Life in Colossians 3:1-17," *RevExp* 70 (1973): 481-93.

0753 Gerald H. Anderson, "Christian Mission and Human Transformation: Toward Century 21," *MS* 2 (1985): 52-65.

relationship to Old Testament
0754 Bernardo M. Antonini, "La conoscenza della volontà di Dio in Col 1,9b," in Antonio Marangon, et al., eds., *La cristologia in san Paolo.* Brescia: Paideia, 1976. Pp. 301-40.

0755 Paul Giem, "σαββάτων in Colossians 2:16," *AUSS* 19 (1981): 195-210.

0756 Pierre Benoit, "Agioi en Colossiens 1:12: hommes ou anges," in Morna Hooker and Stephen Wilson, eds., *Paul and Paulinism.* London: SPCK, 1982. Pp. 83-101.

0757 Kenneth H. Wood, "The 'Sabbath Days' of Colossians 2:16,17," in Kenneth A. Strand, ed., *The Sabbath in Scripture and History.* Washington: Review and Herald Publication Association, 1982. Pp. 338-42.

0758 Pérez Agua, Agustín del, "Derás cristológico del Salmo 110 en el Neuvo Testamento," in Marcos Fernández, et al., eds., *Simposio Biblico Español.* Madrid: Universidad Complutense, 1984. Pp. 637-62.

0759 James D. G. Dunn, "The Colossian Philosophy: A Confident Jewish Apologia," *Bib* 76 (1995): 153-81.

0760 James D. G. Dunn, "Deutero-Pauline Letters," in John M. G. Barclay and John P. M. Sweet, eds., *Early Christian Thought in Its Jewish Context* (festschrift for Morna D. Hooker). New York: Cambridge University Press, 1996. Pp. 130-44.

relation to Philemon

0761 Lamar Cope, "On Rethinking the Philemon-Colossians Connection," *BR* 30 (1985): 45-50.

resurrection

0762 Beda Rigaux, "Col 1,15-20," in *Dieu l'a ressuscité: Exégèse et théologie biblique.* Gembloux: Duculot, 1973. Pp. 154-58.

0763 William L. Craig, "The Historicity of the Empty Tomb of Jesus," *NTS* 31 (1985): 39-67.

0764 Luis F. Ladaria, "Presente y futuro en la escatología cristiana," *EE* 60 (1985): 351-59.

rhetoric

0765 Urban C. Von Wahlde, "Mark 9:33-50: Discipleship: The Authority that Serves," *BZ* NS 29 (1985): 49-67.

0766 Jan Botha, "A Stylistic Analysis of the Christ Hymn (Col 1:15-20)," in Kobus J. H. Petzer and Patrick J. Hartin, eds., *A South African Perspective on the New Testament* (festschrift for Bruce M. Metzger). Leiden: E. J. Brill, 1986. Pp. 238-51.

0767 J. G. van der Watt, "Colossians 1:3-12 Considered as an Exordium," *JTSA* 57 (1986): 32-42.

0768 Jerry L. Sumney, "Those Who 'Pass Judgment': The Identity of the Opponents in Colossians," *Bib* 74 (1993): 366-88.

0769 Harold van Broelhoven, "Persuasion or Praise in Colossians," *EGLMBS* 15 (1995): 65-78.

0770 Thomas H. Olbricht, "The Stoicheia and the Rhetoric of Colossians: Then and Now," in Stanley Porter, et al., eds., *Rhetoric, Scripture and Theology.* Sheffield: JSOT Press, 1996. Pp. 308-28.

righteousness

0771 Gerhard Sauter, "Leiden und 'Handeln'," *EvT* 45 (1985): 435-58.

sex

0772 Ingvild S. Gilhus, "The Gnostic Demiurge: An Agnostic Trickster," *Rel* 14 (1984): 301-11.

0773   LeRoy S. Capper, "The Imago Dei and Its Implications for Order in the Church," *Pres* 11 (1985): 21-33.

sin

0774   Jeffery Gibbs, "The Grace of God as the Foundation for Ethics," *CTQ* 48 (1984): 185-201.

0775   Henri Crouzel, "Die Spiritualität des Origenes: Ihre Bedeutung für die Gegenwart," *TQ* 165 (1985): 132-42.

slavery

0776   Lamar Cope, "On Rethinking the Philemon-Colossians Connection," *BR* 30 (1985): 45-50.

0777   Bernhard Hanssler, "Autorität in der Kirche," *IKaZ* 14 (1985): 493-504.

0778   Mikeal Parsons, "Slavery and the New Testament: Equality and Submissiveness," *VoxE* 18 (1988): 89-96.

0779   Georg Strecker, "Die neutestamentlichen Haustafeln (Kol 3,18-4,1 und Eph 5,22-6,9)," in Helmut Merklein, ed., *Neues Testament und Ethik* (festschrift for Rudolf Schnackenburg). Freiburg: Herder, 1989. Pp. 349-75.

social ethics

0780   Henry I. Lederle, "Better the Devil You Know: Seeking a Biblical Basis for the Societal Dimension of Evil and/or the Demonic in the Pauline Concept of the 'Powers'," in Pieter G. R. De Villiers, ed., *Like a Roaring Lion: Essays on the Bible, the Church and Demonic Powers.* Pretoria: University of South Africa, 1987. Pp. 102-20.

sociology

0781   William R. Herzog, "The 'Household Duties' Passages: Apostolic Traditions and Contemporary Concerns," *Found* 24 (1981): 204-15.

0782   Marlis Giele, "Zur Interpretation der paulinischen Formel τὴν κατ᾽ οἶκον αὐτῆς ἐκκλησίαν," *ZNW* 77 (1986): 109-25.

0783   Stanley J. Samartha, "Religion, Culture and Power - Three Bible Studies," *RS* 34 (1987): 66-79.

0784   R. Scott Nash, "Heuristic Haustafeln: Domestic Codes as Entrance to the Social World of Early Christianity: The Case of Colossians," in Jacob Neusner, et al., eds., *Religious Writings and Religious Systems: Systemic Analysis of Holy Books*. Volume 2. *Christianity*. Atlanta: Scholars Press, 1989. Pp. 25-50.

0785   Wim C. Vergeer, et al., "Die dwaalleer in Kolosse: 'n Konstruksie van die waarskynlike sosio-historiese en filosofiese konteks," *In die Skriflig* 28 (1994): 1-23.

0786   Harold Broeckhoven, "The Social Profiles in the Colossian Debate," *JSNT* 66 (1997): 73-90.

soteriology

0787   R. S. Barbour, "Salvation and Cosmology: The Setting of the Epistle to the Colossians," *SJT* 20 (1967): 257-71.

0788   F.-J. Steinmetz, *Protologische Heils-Zuversicht. Die Strukturen des soteriologischen und christologischen Denkens im Kolosserund Epheserbrief*. Frankfurt: Josef Knecht, 1969.

0789   Eduard Lohse, "Ein hymnisches Bekenntnis in Kol 2,13-15," in A.-L. Descamps and André Halleux, eds., *Mélanges bibliques en hommage au R. P. Béda Rigaux*. Gembloux: Duculot, 1970. Pp. 427-35.

0790   George R. Beasley-Murray, "Second Chapter of Colossians," *RevExp* 70 (1973): 469-79.

0791   Markus Barth, "Christ and All Things," in Morna D. Hooker and Stephen G. Wilson, eds., *Paul and Paulinism* (festschrift for C. K. Barrett). London: SPCK, 1982. Pp. 160-72.

0792   John E. Booty, "Christian Spirituality: From Wilberforce to Temple (Colossians 3:1-3)," in William J. Wolf, ed., *Angican Spirituality*. Wilton CN: Morehouse-Barlow, 1982. Pp. 69-103.

0793   Pierre Benoit, "Pauline Angelology and Demonology: Reflexions on Designations of Heavenly Powers and on Origin of Angelic Evil according to Paul," *RSB* 3 (1983): 1-18.

0794   George Johnston, "Kingdom of God Sayings in Paul's Letters," in Peter Richardson and John C. Hurd, eds., *From Jesus to Paul* (festschrift for Francis W. Beare). Waterloo: Wilfrid Laurier University Press, 1984. Pp. 143-56.

0795 Ambrose Moyo, "The Colossian Heresy in the Light of Some Gnostic Documents from Nag Hammadi," *JTSA* 48 (1984): 30-44.

0796 Walter H. Principe, "The Dignity and Rights of the Human Person as Saved, as Being Saved, as to Be Saved by Christ," *Greg* 65 (1984): 389-430.

0797 Anne Etienne, "Réconciliation: un aspect de la théologie paulinienne," *FV* 84 (1985):49-57.

0798 Mikeal Parsons, "The New Creation," *ET* 99 (1987): 3-4.

0799 Edouard Delebecque, "Sur un probléme de temps chez Saint Paul," - *Bib* 70 (1989): 389-95.

0800 H. Wayne House, "Doctrinal Issues in Colossians," *BSac* 149 (1992): 45-59, 180-92; 151 (1994): 325-38.

0801 Roy Yates, "From Christology to Soteriology," *ET* 107 (1996): 268-70.

source criticism
0802 John W. Wenham, "The Identification of Luke," *EQ* 63 (1991): 3-44.

textual criticism
0803 Ernst Bammel "Versuch zu Col 1:15-20," *ZNW* 52 (1961): 88-95.

0804 I. A. Moir, "The Text of Colossians in Minuscule Manuscripts Housed in Great Britain: Some Preliminary Comments," *StudE* 7 (1982): 355-58.

0805 Pierre Benoit, "Colossiens 2:2-3," in William C. Weinrich, ed., *The New Testament Age* (festschrift for Bo Reicke). 2 vols. Macon GA: Mercer Universitry Press, 1984. 1:41-51.

0806 Markus N. A. Bockmuehl, "A Note on the Text of Colossians 4:3," *JTS* NS 39 (1988): 489-94.

0807 Aidan Breen, "The Liturgical Materials in MS Oxford, Bodleian Library, Auct F4/32," *AL* 34 (1992): 121-53.

0808 Stanley E. Porter, "P Oxy 744.4 and Colossians 3:9," *Bib* 73 (1992): 565-67.

unity

0809 Robert P. Taylor, "Paul's Doctrine of Unity in the Imprisonment Epistles," doctoral dissertation, Southwestern Baptist Theological Seminary, Fort Worth TX, 1939.

wisdom

0810 F.-J. Steinmetz, "Die Weisheit und das Kreuz: Marginalien zum Kolosser- und Epheserbrief," *GeistL* 72 (1998): 112-26.

0811 Robert M. Grant, "The Christ at the Creation," in R. Joseph Hoffmann and Gerald A Larue, eds., *Jesus in History and Myth*. Buffalo NY: Prometheus Books, 1986. Pp. 157-167.

0812 Jarl Fossum, "Colossians 1:15-18a in the Light of Jewish Mysticism and Gnosticism," *NTS* 35 (1989): 183-201.

women

0813 William R. Herzog, "The 'Household Duties' Passages: Apostolic Traditions and Contemporary Concerns," *Found* 24 (1981): 204-15.

0814 Claus Bussmann, "Gibt es christologische Begründungen für eine Unterordnung der Frau im Neuen Testament?" in Gerhard Dautzenberg, et al., eds., *Die Frau im Urchristentum*. Freiburg: Herder, 1983. Pp. 254-62.

0815 Karlheinz Müller, "Die Haustafel des Kolosserbriefes und das antike Frauenthema: Eine kritische Rückschau auf alte Ergebnisse," in Gerhard Dautzenberg, et al., eds., *Die Frau im Urchristentum*. Freiburg: Herder, 1983. Pp. 263-319.

0816 Beverly R. Gaventa, "In Memory of Her: A Review Article," *LTQ* 20 (1985): 58-60.

0817 Wayne Grudem, "Does *Kephale* ('Head') Mean 'Source' or 'Authority over' in Greek Literature: A Survey of 2,336 Examples," *TriJ* NS 6 (1985): 38-59.

0818 W. Stephen Sabom, "The Gnostic World of Anorexia Nervosa," *JPT* 13 (1985): 243-54.

0819   Frank Stagg, "The Gospel, Haustafel, and Women: Mark 1:1;
           Colossians 3:18-4:1," *FM* 2 (1985): 59-63.

0820   Jean Y. Thériault, "La femme chrétienne dans les textes pauliniens,"
           ScE 37 (1985): 297-317.

0821   Robert L. Richardson, "From 'Subjection to Authority' to 'Mutual
           Submission': The Ethic of Subordination in 1 Peter," *FM* 4 (1987):
           70-80.

0822   Anne McGuire, "Equality and Subordination in Christ: Displacing the
           Powers of the Household Code in Colossians," in Joseph Gower, ed.,
           Religion and Economic Ethics. Lanham MD: University Press of
           America, 1990. Pp. 65-85.

0823   John Piper and Wayne A. Grudem, eds., *Recovering Biblical
           Manhood and Womanhood: A Response to Evangelical Feminisma*.
           Wheaton: Crossway Books, 1991.

word studies
0824   A. Vallisoleto, "Delens chirographum," *VD* 12 (1932): 181-85.

0825   J. Huby, "*Stoikeia* dans Bardesane et saint Paul," *Bib* 15 (1934):
           365-68.

0826   Joe B. McMinn, "An Historical Treatment of the Greek Phrase τὰ
           στοιχεῖα (Galatians 4:3 and Colossians 2:8, 20)," doctoral
           dissertation, Southern Baptist Theological Seminary, Louisville KY,
           1950.

0827   O. A. Blanchette, "Does the χειρόγραφον of Colossians 2:14
           Represent Christ Himself," *CBQ* 23 (1961): 306-12.

0828   Johannes L. Witte, "Die Katholizität der Kirche: eine neue Interpre-
           tation nach alter Tradition," *Greg* 42 (1961): 193-241.

0829   Gerhard Münderlein, "Die Erwählung durch das Pleroma--Kol 1:19,"
           NTS 8 (1961-1962): 264-76.

0830   Fred O. Francis, "Humility and Angelic Worship in Colossians 2:18,"
           StTheol 16 (1962): 109-34.

0831 Stanislas Lyonnet, "L'Épître aux Colossiens (Col 2:18) et les mystères d'Apollon Clarien," *Bib* 43 (1962): 417-35.

0832 James H. Burtness, "All the Fulness," *Dia* 3 (1964): 257-63.

0833 G. W. H. Lampe, "New Testament Doctrine of *Ktisis*," *SJT* 17 (1964): 449-62.

0834 Hugolinus Langkammer, "Die Einwohnung der 'absoluten Seinsfülle' in Christus Bemerkungen zu Kol 1,19," *BZ* NS 12 (1968): 258-63.

0835 Lamar Williamson, "Led in Triumph: Paul's Use of *Thriambeuo*," *Int* 22 (1968): 317-32.

0836 Wesley Carr, "Two Notes on Colossians," *JTS* NS 24 (1973): 492-500.

0837 Wolfgang Pöhlmann, "Die hymnischen All-Prädikationen in Kol 1:15-20," *ZNW* 64 (1973): 53-74.

0838 David Schneider, "Colossians 1:15-16 and the Philippine Spirit World," *SEAJT* 15 (1974): 91-101.

0839 Richard J. Bauckham, "Colossians 1:24 Again: The Apocalyptic Motif," *EQ* 47 (1975): 168-70.

0840 Bernardo M. Antonini, "La conoscenza della volontà di Dio in Col 1,9b," in Antonio Marangon, et al., eds., *La cristologia in san Paolo*. Brescia: Paideia, 1976. Pp. 301-40.

0841 Paul Giem, "σαββάτων in Colossians 2:16," *AUSS* 19 (1981): 195-210.

0842 Pierre Benoit, "Agioi en Colossiens 1:12: hommes ou anges," in Morna Hooker and Stephen Wilson, eds., *Paul and Paulinism*. London: SPCK, 1982. Pp. 83-101.

0843 Patrick Rogers, "Hopeful, in Spite of Chains: The Indomitable Spirit of Paul, in the Captivity Letters," *BTB* 12 (1982): 77-81.

0844 Pierre Benoit, "Pauline Angelology and Demonology: Reflexions on Designations of Heavenly Powers and on Origin of Angelic Evil according to Paul," *RSB* 3 (1983): 1-18.

0845   Gedaliahu A. G. Stroumsa, "Form(s) of God: Some Notes on *Metatron* and Christ," *HTR* 76 (1983): 269-88.

0846   F. F. Bruce, "Colossian Problems: The 'Christ Hymn' of Colossians 1:15-20," *BSac* 141 (1984): 99-111.

0847   Ernst Dassmann, "Hausgemeinde und Bischofsamt," in Ernst Dassmann and Klaus Thraede, eds., *Vivarium* (festschrift for Theodor Klauser). Münster, West Germany: Aschendorff, 1984. Pp. 82-97.

0848   Carl Diemer, "Deacons and Other Endangered Species: A Look at the Biblical Office of Deacon," *FundJ* 3 (1984): 21-24.

0849   Carmelo Granado Bellido, "Simbolismo del vestido: interpretación patrística de Gen 49:11," *EE* 59 (1984): 313-57.

0850   Richard D. Patterson, "Christian Patience," *FundJ* 3 (1984): 55.

0851   Jean M. R. Tillard, "What Is the Church of God?" *MidS* 23 (1984): 363-80.

0852   Anne Etienne, "Réconciliation: un aspect de la théologie paulinienne," *FV* 84 (1985):49-57.

0853   Rolf Gögler, "Inkarnationsglaube und Bibeltheologie bei Origenes," *TQ* 165 (1985): 82-94.

0854   Wayne Grudem, "Does *Kephale* ('Head') Mean 'Source' or 'Authority over' in Greek Literature: A Survey of 2,336 Examples," *TriJ* NS 6 (1985): 38-59.

0855   Richard D. Patterson, "Laboring for Christ," *FundJ* 4 (1985): 67.

0856   Galen W. Wiley, "A Study of 'Mystery' in the New Testament," *GTJ* 6 (1985): 349-60.

0857   Roy Yates, "The Worship of Angels," *ET* 97 (1985): 12-15.

0858   Marlis Giele, "Zur Interpretation der paulinischen Formel τὴν κατ᾽ οἶκον αὐτῆς ἐκκλησίαν," *ZNW* 77 (1986): 109-25.

0859 Lars Hartman, "Kroppsligen, 'personligen' eller vad? Till Kol 2:9," *SEÅ* 51-52 (1986): Pp. 72-79.

0860 Gerard S. Sloyan, "Jewish Ritual of the 1st century CE and Christian Sacramental Behavior," *BTB* 15 (1985): 98-103.

0861 Klaus Wengst, "Einander durch Demut für vorzüglicher zu halten: Zum Begriff 'Demut' bei Paulus und in paulinischer Tradition," in Wolfgang Schrage, ed., *Studien zum Text und zur Ethik des Neuen Testaments* (festschrift for Heinrich Greeven). Berlin: Walter de Gruyter, 1986. Pp. 428-39.

0862 Peter T. O'Brien, "The Church as a Heavenly and Eschatological Entity," in Don A. Carson, ed., *The Church in the Bible and the World: An International Study.* Exeter: Paternoster Press, 1987. Pp. 88-119.

0863 Larry R. Helyer, "Arius Revisited: The Firstborn over All Creation," *JETS* 31 (1988): 59-67.

0864 Antonio Orbe, "Deus facit, homo fit: un axioma de san Ireneo," *Greg* 69 (1988): 629-61.

0865 Eduard Schweizer, "Slaves of the Elements and Worshipers of Angels," *JBL* 107 (1988): 455-68.

0866 Eduard Schweizer, "Altes und Neues zu den 'Elementen der Welt' in Kol 2,20; Gal 4,3-9," in Kurt Aland and Siegfried Meurer, eds., - *Wissenschaft und Kirche* (festschrift for Eduard Lohse). Bielefeld: Luther-Verlag, 1989. Pp. 111-18.

0867 Michelangelo Tabet, "I testi paolini sulla paradosis nei commenti patristici," in Willy Rordorf, et al., eds., *La tradizione: forme e modi: XVIII Incontro di studiosi dell'antichità cristiana.* Rome: Institutum Patristicum Augustinianum, 1990. Pp. 39-53.

0868 Roy Yates, "Colossians 2:14: Metaphor of Forgiveness," *Bib* 71 (1990): 248-59.

0869 John W. Wenham, "The Identification of Luke," *EQ* 63 (1991): 3-44.

0870 Dietrich Rusam, "Neue Belege zu den stoicheia tou kosmou," *ZNW* 83 (1992): 119-25.

0871   Troy Martin, "But Let Everyone Discern the Body of Christ," *JBL*
        114 (1995): 249-55.

0872   Troy Martin, "The Scythian Perspective in Colossians 3:11," *NovT* 37
        (1995): 249-61.

0873   Douglas A. Campbell, "Unravelling Colossians 3:11b," *NTS* 42
        (1996): 120-32.

0874   Robert J. Karris, *A Symphony of New Testament Hymns: Commentary
        on Philippians 2:5-11, Colossians 1:15-20, Ephesians 2:14-16, 1
        Timothy 3:16, Titus 3:4-7, 1 Peter 3:18-22, and 2 Timothy 2:11-13.*
        Collegeville MN: Liturgical Press, 1996.

0875   Thomas H. Olbricht, "The Stoicheia and the Rhetoric of Colossians:
        Then and Now," in Stanley E. Porter and Thomas H. Olbricht, eds.,
        Rhetoric, Scripture and Theology. Sheffield: Sheffield Academic
        Press, 1996. Pp. 308-28.

0876   Douglas A. Campbell, "The Scythian Perspective in Colossians 3:11:
        A Response to Troy Martin," *NovT* 39 (1997): 81-84.

0877   Gene R. Smillie, "Ephesians 6:19-20: A Mystery for the Sake of
        Which the Apostle is an Ambassador in Chains," *TriJ* 18 (1997):
        199-222.

0878   C. Basevi, "Col 1:15-20: Las posibles fuentes del 'himmo'
        cristológico y su importamcia para la interpretación," *ScripT* 30
        (1998): 779-802.

0879   E. Krentz, "κατὰ τὸν χριστόν: Preaching Colossians in Year C,"
        CThM 25 (1998): 132-36.

worship
        0880   Charles D. Taylor, "A Comparative Study of the Concept of Worship
        in Colossians and Hebrews," doctoral dissertation, Southern Baptist
        Theological Seminary, Louisville KY, 1957.

PART THREE

Commentaries

0881 G. Currie Martin, *Ephesians, Colossians, Philemon, & Philippians*. The New Century Bible. New York: H. Frowde, 1902.

0882 Albert B. Simpson, *Philippians, Colossians, Thessalonians*. New York: Alliance Press, 1903.

0883 H. J. C. Knight, *The Epistles of Paul the Apostle to the Colossians and to Philemon*. London: Methuen, 1907.

0884 A. Lukyn Williams, *The Epistles of Paul the Apostle to the Colossians and to Philemon*. Cambridge Greek Testament for Schools and Colleges. Cambridge UK: University Press, 1907.

0885 G. Alexander, *The Epistles to the Colossians and to the Ephesians*. New York: Macmillan, 1910.

0886 S. R. Macphail, *The Epistle of Paul to the Colossians*. Edinburgh: T. & T. Clark, 1911.

0887 Joseph Knabenbauer, *Commentarius in S. Pauli apostoli epistolas. IV, Epistolae ad Ephesios ad Philippenses et ad Colossenses*. Cursus Scripturae Sacrae #2/4. Parisiis: Sumptibus P. Lethielleux, 1912.

0888 W. L. Walker, *Christ the Creative Ideal: Studies in Colossians and Ephesians*. Edinburgh: T. & T. Clark, 1913.

0889 Frederick B. Westcott, *A Letter to Asia: Being a Paraphrase and Brief Exposition of the Epistle of Paul the Apostle to the Believers at Colossae*. London: Macmillan, 1914.

0890 T. K. Abbott, *A Critical and Exegetical Commentary on the Epistles to the Ephesians and to the Colossians*. ICC. New York: Charles Scribner's Sons, 1916.

0891 Constant Toussaint, *L'Épître de S. Paul aux Colossiens: traduction et commentaire*. Paris: Emile Nourry, 1921.

0892 Walter K. Firminger, *The Epistles of St. Paul the Apostle to the Colossians and to Philemon*. London: SPCK, 1921.

0893 Fritz Horn, *Der Brief an die Kolosser*. Krefeld: Druck und Verlag des Korrespondenzblattes der freunde des Heidelberger Katechismus, 1926.

0894 A. T. Robertson, *Paul and the Intellectuals: The Epistle to the Colossians*. Garden City NY: Doubleday, 1928.

0895 Ernest F. Scott, *The Epistles of Paul to the Colossians, to Philemon and to the Ephesians.* New York: R. R. Smith, 1930.

0896 Lewis B. Radford, *The Epistle to the Colossians and the Epistle to Philemon.* London: Methuen, 1931.

0897 Charles R. Erdman, *The Epistles of Paul to the Colossians and to Philemon: An Exposition.* Philadelphia, The Westminster Press, 1933.

0898 E. Y. Mullins, *Studies in Colossians.* Nashville: Broadman Press, 1935.

0899 Werner Bieder, *Der Kolosserbrief.* Schweizerisches Bibelwerk für die Gemeinde. Zurich: Zwingli, 1943.

0900 Bede Frost, *Ephesians, Colossians: A Dogmatic and Devotional Commentary.* London: Mowbray, 1946.

0901 R. C. H. Lenski, *The Interpretation of St. Paul's Epistles to the Colossians, to the Thessalonians, to the Timothy, to Titus and to Philemon.* Columbus: Wartburg Press, 1946.

0902 Crete Gray, *The Epistles of St. Paul to the Colossians and Philemon.* London: Lutterworth Press, 1948.

0903 Pierre Bonnard, *L'Épître de Saint Paul aux Philippiens.* Neuchatel: Delachaux & Niestlé, 1950.

0904 C. Masson, *L'Épître de Saint Paul aux Colossiens.* Paris: Delachaux & Niestlé, 1950.

0905 Otto H. Schmidt, *Saint Paul Shows Us How: St. Paul's Epistle to Colossians.* St. Louis: Concordia Publishing House, 1950.

0906 Fritz Pfeil, *Der Kolosserbrief.* Stuttgart: Kreuz-Verlag, 1951.

0907 Francis C. Synge, *Philippians and Colossians: Introduction and Commentary.* London: SCM Press, 1951.

0908 Martin Dibelius and Heinrich Greeven, *An die Kolosser, Epheser, an Philemon.* Tübingin: Mohr, 1953.

0909 William Hendriksen, *New Testament Commentary.* Grand Rapids: Baker, 1953.

0910 Kenneth S. Wuest, *Ephesians and Colossians in the Greek New Testament for the English Reader*. Grand Rapids: Eerdmans, 1953.

0911 Werner de Boor, *Die Briefe des Paulus an die Philipper und an die Kolosser*. Wuppertal: Brockhaus, 1957.

0912 C. F. D. Moule, *The Epistles of Paul the Apostle to the Colossians and to Philemon: An Introduction and Commentary*. Cambridge Greek Testament Commentary. Cambridge: University Press, 1957.

0913 Edmund K. Simpson, *Commentary on the Epistles to the Ephesians and the Colossians*. Grand Rapids MI: Eerdmans 1957.

0914 Pierre Benoit, *Les épîtres de saint Paul aux Philippiens, à Philémon, aux Colossiens, aux Éphésiens*. Paris: Cerf, 1959.

0915 A. M. Hunter, *The Letter of Paul to the Galatians; the Letter of Paul to the Ephesians; the Letter of Paul to the Philippians; the Letter of Paul to the Colossians*. Richmond VA: John Knox Press, 1959.

0916 Karl Staab, *Die Thessalonicherbriefe. Die Gefangenschaftsbriefe* Regensburg: Friedrich Pustet, 1959.

0917 Herbert M. Carson, *The Epistles of Paul to the Colossians and Philemon: An Introduction and Commentary*. The Tyndale New Testament Commentaries. Grand Rapids: Eerdmans, 1960.

0918 Herman N. Ridderbos, *Aan de Kolossenzen*. Kampen: J. H. Kok, 1960.

0919 Earl C. Smith, *Paul's Gospel: An Analysis and Exposition of Paul's Epistles to the Romans, to the Galatians, to the Ephesians, to the Phillippians, to the Colossians*. New York: Greenwich Book Publishers, 1960.

0920 Louis J. Baggott, *A New Approach to Colossians*. London: A. R. Mowbray, 1961.

0921 Ernst Lohmeyer, *Die Briefe an die Kolosser und an Philemon*. Göttingen: Vandenhoeck & Ruprecht, 1961.

0922 Oliver B. Greene, *The Epistle of Paul the Apostle to the Colossians*. Greenville SC: Gospel Hour, 1963.

0923 H. K. Moulton, *Colossians, Philemon, and Ephesians*. London: Epworth Press, 1963.

0924 Adolf Schlatter, *Die Briefe an Die Galater, Epheser, Kolosser und Philemon*. Stuttgart: Calver Verlag, 1963.

0925 Horst Bannach, *Der Himmel ist nicht mehr oben: Probleme des 20. Jahrhunderts im Spiegel des Kolosserbriefs*. Stuttgart: Quell, 1964.

0926 Olof Linton, *Pauli mindre brev*. Stockholm: Diakonistyrelsens Bokforlag, 1964.

0927 Ferdinand Sigg, *Jesus Christus herrscht als Konig: eine Erklarung des Kolosserbriefes*. Zurich: Gotthelf-Verlaf, 1964.

0928 J. E. Uitman, *De Brief van Paulus aan de Colossenzen*. De Prediking van het Nieuwe Testament. Nijkerk: G. F. Callenbach, 1964.

0929 Franz Mussner, *Der brief an die Kolosser: Geistliche Schriftlesung*. Erlauterungen zum Neuen Testament für die Geistliche Lesung #12. Dusseldorf: Patmos-Verlag, 1965.

0930 Udo Borse, *Der Kolosserbrieftext des Pelagius*. Bonn: Rheinische Friedrich-Wilhelms-Universitat, 1966.

0931 George Johnston, *Ephesians, Philippians, Colossians and Philemon*. London: Nelson, 1967.

0932 Nikolaus Kehl, *Der Christushymnus im Kolosserbrief; eine motivgeschichtliche Untersuchung, zu Kol. 1,12-20*. Stuttgart: Verlag Katholisches Bibelwerk, 1967.

0933 G. H. P. Thompson, *The Letters of Paul to the Ephesians, to the Colossians and to Philemon*. London: Cambridge University Press, 1967.

0934 Norbert Hugedé, *Commentaire de l'Épître aux Colossiens*. Genève: Labor et fides, 1968.

0935 Ludwig Schmidt, *Epheser und Kolosser*. Stuttgart: E. Klotz, 1970.

0936 Everett F. Harrison, *Colossians: Christ All-Sufficient*. Everyman's Bible Commentary. Chicago: Moody Press, 1971.

0937 Eduard Lohse, *Colossians and Philemon: A Commentary on the Epistles to the Colossians and to Philemon*. Hermeneia. Philadelphia: Fortress Press, 1971.

0938 Michael R. Weed, *The Letters of Paul to the Ephesians, the Colossians, and Philemon*. Austin: R. B. Sweet, 1971.

0939 Thomas J. Barling, *The Letter to the Colossians*. Birmingham: Christadelphian, 1972.

0940 Gilbert Bouwman, *De brieven van Paulus aan de Kolossenzen en aan Filemon*. Roermond: Romen, 1972.

0941 Ralph P. Martin, *Colossians: The Church's Lord and the Christian's Liberty: An Expository Commentary with a Present-day Application*. Exeter UK: Paternoster Press, 1972.

0942 Ralph P. Martin, *Colossians and Philemon: Based on the Revised Standard Version*. New century Bible Commentary. Grand Rapids: Eerdmans, 1973.

0943 Josef Ernst, *Die Briefe an die Philipper, an Philemon, an die Kolosser, an die Epheser*. Regensburg: Pustet, 1974.

0944 Philippe Favre, *L'Épître aux Colossiens*. Geneve: La Maison de la Bible, 1974.

0945 Jürgen Becker, Hans Conzelmann and G. Friedrich, *Die Brief an die Galater, Epheser, Philipper, Kolosser, Thessalonicher und Philemon*. NTD #8. Göttingen: Vandenhoeck & Ruprecht, 1976.

0946 G. B. Caird, *Paul's Letters from Prison: Ephesians, Philippians, Colossians, Philemon*. Oxford: Oxford University Press, 1976.

0947 Robert G. Bratcher and Eugene A. Nida, *A Translator's Handbook on Paul's Letters to the Colossians and to Philemon*. London: United Bible Societies, 1977.

0948 James L. Houlden, *Paul's Letters from Prison: Philippians, Colossians, Philemon, and Ephesians*. Philadelphia: Westminster Press, 1977.

0949 Lloyd J. Ogilvie, *Loved and Forgiven*. Glendale CA: Regal Books, 1977.

0950 Sandor Cserhati, *Pal apostolnak a kolossebeliekhez irt levele es Filemonhoz irt levele*. Budapest: Magyarorszagi Evangelikus Egyhaz Sajtoosztalya, 1978.

0951 J. Paul Sampley, *Ephesians, Colossians, 2 Thessalonians, the Pastoral Epistles*. Philadelphia: Fortress Press, 1978.

0952 Gary W. Demarest, *Colossians: The Mystery of Christ in Us*. Waco TX: Word Books, 1979.

0953 J. Gnilka, *Der Kolosserbrief*. HNT 10. Freiburg, Herder, 1980.

0954 R. C. Lucas, *Fullness and Freedom: The Message of Colossians and Philemon*. Downers Grove IL: InterVarsity Press, 1980.

0955 H. D. McDonald, *Commentary on Colossians and Philemon*. Waco TX: Word, 1980.

0956 Patrick Rogers, *Colossians*. New Testament Message #15. Wilmington DL: M. Glazier, 1980.

0957 C. Vaughan, *Colossians and Philemon*. Bible Study Commentary. Grand Rapids, Zondervan, 1980.

0958 Robert G. Gromacki, *Stand Perfect in Wisdom: An Exposition of Colossians and Philemon*. Grand Rapids: Baker Book House, 1981.

0959 Manford G. Gutzke, *Plain Talk on Colossians*. Grand Rapids: Zondervan, 1981.

0960 James T. Draper, *Colossians: A Portrait of Christ*. Wheaton IL: Tyndale House Publishers, 1982.

0961 Maxie D. Dunnam, *Galatians, Ephesians, Philippians, Colossians, Philemon*. Waco TX: Word, 1982.

0962 H. A. Ironside, *Philippians, Colossians, Thessalonians*. Neptune NJ: Loizeaux Brothers, 1982.

0963 Peter T. O'Brien, *Colossians, Philemon*. Word Biblical Commentary #44. Waco TX: Word, 1982.

0964 Eduard Schweizer, *The Letter to the Colossians: A Commentary*. Minneapolis: Augsburg, 1982.

0965 Ivan Havener, *First Thessalonians, Philippians, Philemon, Second Thessalonians, Colossians, Ephesians.* Collegeville MN: Liturgical Press, 1983.

0966 Andreas Lindemann, *Der Kolosserbrief.* Zurcher Bibelkommentare #10. Zurich: Theologischer Verlag, 1983.

0967 Arthur G. Patzia, *Colossians, Philemon, Ephesians.* San Francisco: Harper & Row, 1984.

0968 John A. Knight, et al., *Philippians, Colossians, Philemon.* Kansas City MO: Beacon Hill Press, 1985.

0969 John H. Reumann and Walter F. Taylor, *Ephesians / Colossians.* Augsburg Commentary on the New Testament. Minneapolis: Augsburg Publishing House, 1985.

0970 Joseph Comblin, *Epístola aos colossenses e epístola a filêmon.* Vozes: Editora Sinodal, 1986.

0971 N. T. Wright, *The Epistles of Paul to the Colossians and to Philemon: An Introduction and Commentary.* The Tyndale New Testament Commentaries. Grand Rapids: Eerdmans, 1986.

0972 Geoffrey C. Bingham, *The Fulness of Christ: The Epistle to the Colossians.* Blackwood, South Australia: New Creation, 1987.

0973 Daniel Furter, *Les épîtres de Paul aux Colossiens et à Philemon.* Vaux-sur-Seine, France: EDIFAC, 1987.

0974 Rudolf Hoppe, *Epheserbrief, Kolosserbrief.* Stuttgarter kleiner Kommentar #10. Stuttgart: Katholisches Bibelwerk, 1987.

0975 Josef Pfammatter, *Epheserbrief, Kolosserbrief.* Die neue Echter Bibel. Würzburg: Echter Verlag, 1987.

0976 P. Pokorný, *Der Brief des Paulus an die Kolosser* Theologischer Handkommentar zum Neuen Testament #10. Berlin: Evangelische Verlagsanstalt, 1987.

0977 Eduard Schick, *Der erloste Kosmos: eine geistliche, gegenwartsbezogene Auslegung des Kolosserbriefes.* Stuttgart: Verlag Katholisches Bibelwerk, 1987.

0978   Thomas Marberry, *Galatians through Colossians*. Nashville: Randall House
Publications, 1988.

0979   Gary Weedman, *Philippians--Thessalonians: Unlocking the Scriptures for
You*. Cincinnati: Standard Publications, 1988.

0980   R. Kent Hughes, *Colossians and Philemon: The Supremacy of Christ*.
Westchester IL: Crossway Books, 1989.

0981   Carol K. Stockhausen, *Letters in the Pauline Tradition: Ephesians,
Colossians, I Timothy, II Timothy, and Titus*. Message of Biblical Spirituality
#13. Wilmington DL: Glazier, 1989.

0982   David K. Bernard, *The Message of Colossians and Philemon*. Hazelwood
MO: Word Aflame Press, 1990.

0983   Murray J. Harris, *Colossians & Philemon*. Grand Rapids: Eerdmans, 1991.

0984   Richard R. Melick, *Philippians, Colossians, Philemon*. The New American
Commentary #32. Nashville: Broadman Press, 1991.

0985   John MacArthur, *Colossians & Philemon*. Chicago: Moody Press, 1992.

0986   Heiko Krimmer, *Kolosserbrief*. Neuhausen-Stuttgart: Hanssler, 1992.

0987   Ralph P. Martin, *Ephesians, Colossians, and Philemon*. Louisville: John
Knox Press, 1992.

0988   Georges Gander, *Les épîtres de Paul aux Colossiens et aux Philippiens:
nouveau commentaire d'après l'arameen, le grec et le latin*. Saint-Legier,
Suisse: Editions Contrastes, 1993.

0989   Gerhard Krodel, *The Deutero-Pauline Letters: Ephesians, Colossians, 2
Thessalonians, 1-2 Timothy, Titus*. Minneapolis: Fortress Press, 1993.

0990   Ernest D. Martin, *Colossians, Philemon*. Believers Church Bible
Commentary. Scottdale PA: Herald Press, 1993.

0991   Robert W. Wall, *Colossians & Philemon*. The IVP New Testament
Commentary Series. Downers Grove IL: InterVarsity Press, 1993.

0992 Michael Wolter, *Der Brief an die Kolosser: Der Brief an Philemon*. Okumenischer Taschenbuchkommentar zum Neuen Testament #12. Gütersloh: Gütersloher Verlagshaus, 1993.

0993 Roy Yates, *The Epistle to the Colossians*. Epworth Commentaries. London: Epworth Press, 1993.

0994 J-N. Aletti, *Lettera ai Colossei: introduzione, versione, commento*. Bologna: EDB, 1994.

0995 Anthony L. Ash, *Philippians, Colossians & Philemon*. Joplin MO: College Press, 1994.

0996 Markus Barth, *Colossians: A New Translation with Introduction and Commentary*. New York: Doubleday, 1994.

0997 Bruce B. Barton, *Philippians, Colossians, Philemon*. Wheaton IL: Tyndale House Publishers, 1995.

0998 Bonnie B. Thurston, *Reading Colossians, Ephesians, and 2 Thessalonians: A Literary and Theological Commentary*. New York: Crossroad, 1995.

0999 Lewis R. Donelson, *Colossians, Ephesians, First and Second Timothy, and Titus*. Westminster Bible Companion. Louisville: Westminster/John Knox Press, 1996.

1000 James D. G. Dunn, *The Epistles to the Colossians and to Philemon: A Commentary on the Greek Text*. Grand Rapids: Eerdmans, 1996.

1001 Daniel J. Harrington, *Paul's Prison Letters: Spiritual Commentaries on Paul's Letters to Philemon, the Philippians, and the Colossians*. Spiritual Commentaries. Hyde Park NY: New City Press, 1997.

1002 Hans Hübner, *An Philemon, an die Kolosser, an die Epheser*. Handbuch zum Neuen Testament #12. Tübingen: Mohr, 1997.

1003 David E. Garland, *Colossians and Philemon*. The NIV Application Commentary. Grand Rapids: Zondervan, 1998.

1004 C. R. Hume, *Reading through Colossians and Ephesians*. London: SCM Press, 1998.

1005   Adrienne von Speyr, *The Letter to the Colossians*. San Francisco: Ignatius Press, 1998.

Index

Bruce, F. F.   0094, 0419, 0538, 0604,
    0645, 0683, 0717, 0746, 0846,
Buls, Harold H.   0236
Bunkowske, Eugene W.   0167, 0726
Burger, C.   0072, 0073, 0588, 0589
Bürke, H.   0054
Burtness, James H.   0051, 0401, 0575,
    0832
Bussmann, Claus   0359, 0412, 0814
Cahill, Michael   0170
Caird, G. B.   0946
Cambouropoulos, P.   0668
Camelot, T.   0294
Campbell, Douglas A.   0330, 0331,
    0873, 0876
Cannon, G. E.   0682
Cantalamessa, R.   0132
Capper, LeRoy S.   0324, 0773
Carr, Wesley   0248, 0269, 0836
Carson, Herbert M.   0917
Catherwood, Fred   0360, 0490
Chester, Andrew   0117, 0388, 0430
Christopher, Gregory T.   0259, 0457
Cipriani, Settimio   0153
Clifford, Richard J.   0119, 0448
Cockran, Dan   0511
Comblin, Joseph   0970
Combrink, V.   0459
Cone, Orello   0616
Conzelmann, Hans   0945
Cope, Lamar   0367, 0556, 0761, 0776
Coughenour, Robert A.   0230
Coutts, J.   0633
Craddock, Fred B.   0058, 0403, 0579
Craig, William L.   0242, 0730, 0763
Crespy, G.   0292
Crouch, James E.   0526
Crouzel, Henri   0018, 0137, 0775
Cserhati, Sandor   0950
Dacquino, P.   0076, 0149, 0171, 0592,
    0649
Dassmann, Ernst   0377, 0847
de Ausejo, S.   0044, 0567
de Boor, Werner   0911
de Ru, G.   0681
Deichgräber, R.   0060, 0580

del Pérez Agua, A.   0299, 0417, 0758
Delebecque, Edouard   0300, 0799
Demarest, Gary W.   0952
DeMaris, Richard E.   0702
Dettwiler, Andreas   0704
di Giovanni, A.   0077, 0593
Dibelius, Martin   0908
Diemer, Carl   0012, 0188, 0848
Dockx, S.   0671
Donelson, Lewis R.   0999
Drake, Alfred E.   0396
Draper, James T.   0960
Dschulnigg, Peter   0697
Du Plessis, Isak J.   0431
Dulap, Willis   0216, 0279, 0322
Duncan, George S.   0621, 0630
Dunn, James D. G.   0385, 0433, 0707,
    0759, 0760, 1000
Dunnam, Maxie D.   0961
Durrwell, F.-X.   0034
Efrid, J. M.   0461, 0676
Egan, R. B.   0254
Ellingworth, Paul   0050, 0574
Ellis, E. E.   0374
Erdman, Charles R.   0897
Ernst, J.   0157, 0221
Ernst, Josef   0943
Esser, Hans H.   0135, 0321
Etienne, Anne   0100, 0748, 0797, 0852
Evans, H.   0376
Evans, Craig A.   0536
Favre, Philippe   0944
Ferguson, Evertt   0234, 0442
Feuillet, André   0128, 0145, 0404
Firminger, Walter K.   0892
Flemington, W. F.   0182
Flint, Thomas   0701
Förster, Werner   0046, 0510, 0569,
    0647
Fossum, Jarl   0108, 0521, 0812
Francis, Fred O.   0267, 0566, 0669,
    0830
Frautschi, Emanuel   0636
Fretheim, Terence E.   0141
Friedrich, G.   0945
Frost, Bede   0900

Munn, Gene L.   0512, 0661
Munro, Winsome   0344
Mussner, Franz   0101, 0421, 0483, 0715, 0929
Nash, R. Scott   0354, 0562, 0784
Nida, Eugene A.   0947
Nielsen, Charles M.   0685
Noyen, C.   0658
O'Brien, Peter T.   0161, 0286, 0469, 0484, 0586, 0742, 0862, 0963
O'Neill, J.   0013, 0205
Ochel, Werner   0620
Ogara, F.   0037, 0334
Ogilvie, Lloyd J.   0949
Olbricht, Thomas H.   0770, 0874, 0875
Orbe, Antonio   0104, 0520, 0864
Panimolle, S. A.   0159
Paradis, H.   0638
Parsons, Mikeal   0325, 0328, 0778, 0798
Patterson, Richard D.   0160, 0191, 0337, 0733, 0850, 0855
Patzia, Arthur G.   0967
Penna, Romano   0304
Percy, E.   0624, 0626
Perret, Jean   0020, 0203, 0290
Perriman, Andrew C.   0186, 0432
Peters, Ted   0390
Peterson, Robert A.   0164, 0734
Pfammatter, Josef   0975
Pfeil, Fritz   0906
Pfitzner, V. C.   0195
Pickering, Wilbur N.   0677
Pierce, Rice A.   0373
Piper, John   0725, 0823
Piper, O. A.   0014
Pöhlmann, Wolfgang   0068, 0585, 0837
Pokorný, P.   0976
Polhill, John B.   0662
Pollard, T. Evan   0025, 0134, 0411
Porter, Stanley E.   0318, 0808
Principe, Walter H.   0327, 0492, 0796
Radford, Lewis B.   0896
Ramaroson, L.   0008
Read, David H. C.   0306, 0422
Reicke, Bo   0283, 0663
Reumann, John H. P.   0187, 0737, 0969

Rey, B.   0312, 0313
Richardson, Robert L.   0351, 0821
Ridderbos, Herman N.   0918
Rigaux, Beda   0069, 0762
Roberts, J. H.   0036, 0691
Robertson, A. T.   0894
Robinson, J. M.   0045, 0568
Rodd, C. S.   0212
Rogers, Patrick   0552, 0843, 0956
Rollins, Wayne G.   0514
Rossano, P.   0081, 0597
Roth, Robert Paul   0004, 0206
Rowland, Christopher   0386, 0414
Rusam, Dietrich   0219, 0282, 0534, 0870
Rutherford, John   0618
Sabom, W. Stephen   0260, 0340, 0518, 0818
Sabourin, Leopold   0017, 0166, 0309, 0464, 0732
Sacchi, A.   0162
Samartha, Stanley J.   0019, 0241, 0783
Sampley, J. Paul   0951
Sanders, E. P.   0648
Sanders, J. T.   0064, 0583
Sappington, Thomas J.   0389, 0751
Sauter, Gerhard   0184, 0495, 0731, 0771
Scharf, Kurt   0057, 0402, 0750
Schenk, Wolfgang   0092, 0415, 0603
Schick, Eduard   0977
Schille, G.   0220, 0578, 0675
Schlatter, Adolf   0924
Schmidt, Ludwig   0935
Schmidt, Otto H.   0905
Schmithals, Walter   0537
Schnackenberg, Gjertrud   0692
Schnackenburg, R.   0030, 0190, 0308
Schneider, David   0130, 0838
Schweer, G. William   0524
Schweizer, Eduard   0067, 0102, 0105, 0114, 0185, 0214, 0217, 0271, 0276, 0278, 0280, 0281, 0407, 0423, 0446, 0447, 0530, 0531, 0544, 0632, 0664, 0672, 0673, 0865, 0866, 0964
Scott, Ernest F.   0895

Wiley, Galen W.   0189, 0856
Williams, A. Lukyn   0884
Williamson, Lamar   0253, 0835
Willmington, Harold L.   0237, 0547
Wilson, Walter T.   0504
Wink, Walter   0115, 0429, 0693
Witte, Johannes L.   0154, 0460, 0828
Wolter, Michael   0992
Wood, Kenneth H.   0261, 0757
Wright, N. T.   0116, 0416, 0477, 0971

Wuest, Kenneth S.   0910
Wulf, F.   0302
Yates, Roy   0178, 0250, 0251, 0257,
   0270, 0287, 0435, 0450, 0454,
   0519, 0540, 0565, 0678, 0728,
   0801, 0857, 0868, 0993
Young, Francis   0500
Zabala, Artemio M.   0112
Zedda, S.   0181
Zeillinger, F.   0002, 0070